General Introduction

Dramawork is a continuation of the ideas put forward in our collection *Exploration Drama*. The basic material and approach of that series is the foundation of the ideas developed here. In *Dramawork* we suggest some beginnings of ideas which can be taken and filled out, or which can be used as a starting point for completely different ideas. *Dramawork* is work in progress, or looked at in another way—play. *Dramawork* centres on several approaches and attitudes to drama.

Fun : Drama for enjoyment before anything else. Such drama has no difficult rules, no exacting standards. It is primarily fun to do.

Finding Out : A method of understanding people and places and events. This can require considerable research into original source material of many kinds. It may be necessary to study historical documents or to hunt for old ballads in order to gather information which can form the basis of a script.

A Skill : A development of the skills of drama, researching into the precision and exactitude drama can demand of an individual or a group.

A Presentation : A display of findings to an audience—either as a play or in some other form.

An Audience : Watching somebody else's work. The free interplay of criticism between audience and actors is vital to the development of all dramatic work.

The most important thing about the drama considered here, is that it should be free. It shouldn't have to follow any known routes, and should take off on its own journey, depending on who is doing it.

The basic unit working together is considered as 'the group'—the teacher or organiser is 'the leader', but is an integral part of the group.

Experiments and exploration of the uses of sound, lighting and design are aspects of group work in drama. There is no real need for rigid specialisation unless a specific group or project demands it.

Introduction to Book Two

The material in this book is concerned with exploring some avenues of drama, with a more detailed consideration of work which is to be presented. It is impossible and undesirable to set standards which are constant on dramawork. But there must be standards, and one important aspect of drama is the study and work on plays and scripts, and the development of forms of drama from within the group.

A play may be used in different ways, it can be read, acted, performed, discussed, used as a basis for improvisation, analysed or re-written. But it will have first been conceived in terms of performance, and it is in the performance of drama that its achievement largely lies.

Because the roots of drama exist in human activity and thought, the presentation of plays can only be a culmination of an experience of activity and thought, which must always be present in work in drama. It is senseless to attempt ideas which do not relate to the experience of the group, either in terms of imaginative and physical capacity or in terms of what the group enjoy. Some groups may never reach the stage of wanting to present their work, although out of presentational ideas they find a fund of material suitable for exploration and fun.

workshop

a. Drama productions
b. Offshoots

a. Drama productions

Space

Drama needs space. The actual space itself depends on the needs of the group, and no rules can be laid down. People can function, and function well, in a space in which they feel comfortable, and which they enjoy. It should be equipped with some stage lights, and have one or more dimmer boards, ropes, pulleys and rostra blocks. It should have a main space which is always used for action, and ancillary spaces for making things, for painting and for relaxing. Some suggestions are given in *Dramawork 1*.

A clear space is all that is necessary. Its size and shape will determine how it is used. A raised platform at one end, for example, can be used as a stage, as a level in the action, a height for jumping from, a place to put spectators, or just ignored.

Reference

HMSO Building Bulletin 30, Secondary School Design.

Theatre in the Round Stephen Joseph, Barrie & Rockliffe

Actor and Architect Stephen Joseph, Manchester University Press

Design

Out of the needs of the group will come functional aspects of design. Questions need to be asked:

What work is going to be done in the space?

What is the aim of such work? (Is it for different groups to work in? Is it for formal work? Is it for presentations with audiences?)

Is there enough light, heat, room, for this group?

Is there provision for technical apparatus, pictures, costumes, books?

Is it possible to work, see, hear, without constant interruption?

Spaces, such as can be found, in old huts, isolated rooms, discarded church halls, etc., are adaptable as drama spaces. How the space is used will depend upon the group and its needs.

Visual aspects of design are complementary to the functional. What is it to look like? An old hut will need re-decorating to make it pleasant and workable. It is difficult to pin down a standard. It is a question of needs and taste. Drama is action (in space) and it is also a visual experience. It therefore needs designing. Design plays a dual role—functional and visual. It involves the actor and the spectator. Design must unite the visual and functional aspects of the action, and it therefore stems from within the dynamic of the drama.

Experiments

Exploring the nature of dramatic activity using all forms of the allied arts, involving the use of different materials (plastics, wood, metal, paper, cardboard, textiles, etc.), different aspects of light (spotlights, floodlights, daylight, film, slides, shadows, etc.), different aspects of sound (amplified sound, distorted sound, vocal variations, music, etc.), the use of the body (dance, gymnastics, movement, etc.), and the use of the written word.

Games

'Free' drama involving acting games, street games, children's games and improvisation. This suggests an open space, or an environment which is totally used (climbing over whatever obstacles, platforms and rostra there are).

Plays

Formal written scripts which are a complete work by an author. Each play has its own identity and nature, which should be interpreted as much in the design as in other aspects.

Social drama

Exploring aspects of ourselves as people and the world we live in. This suggests a use of modern communication-techniques, such as the camera, the newspaper, the television and the tape recorder. The design of such media, as well as domestic objects, architecture and transport, will affect attitudes to design in drama. Space and equipment should be available for reproduction of photographs, films, magazines and recordings.

Ritual

One of the basic elements of drama. Dynamic, organised but spontaneous within a framework, the ritualistic/religious roots of drama come through much of the spectacular element in drama, and reflect other basic elements such as conflict, contrast, atmosphere, suspense, concentration, and climax.

It is impossible to separate the aims of a drama work from its design, they are aspects of the same thing. Sometimes it is necessary to construct a totally new environment—such is the nature of stage scenery, which is an attempt to appear to change the location through design. Although elaborate scenery is almost always unnecessary, an arrangement of units and shapes, decorated either with paint or with textures and colours, is a traditional way of effecting the required change. Different ages have discovered different solutions, and films, slides, artificial lighting, and methods of breaking up the acting area are used as well as flat areas of canvas and rostra blocks.

Reference

Basic Design M. Sausmarez, Studio Vista
The Nature of Design D. Pye, Studio Vista
Stage Design K. Rowell, Studio Vista
Designing and Making Stage Scenery M. Warre, Studio Vista

Theatre—the ideas of three producers.

The Greeks had large open-air productions, the middle ages: street performances on portable platforms, the Elizabethans: stages thrusting into the audience, the Victorians: picture-frame stages separated from the audience, and several places today have the audience all the way round the action. There is a great variety of methods of presenting drama productions. How a particular production is approached depends partly on the conviction of the producer, the person responsible for organising and putting on the play. Here are some extracts from comments by three twentieth century producers, which show their attitudes to the staging of plays. There are many others, but each reveals the conviction necessary to the production of a play.

Antonin Artaud (1896–1948)
The means, which consist of intensities of colours, lights, or sounds, which utilise vibrations, tremors, repetition, whether of a musical rhythm or a spoken phrase, special tones or a general diffusion of light.

So composed and so constructed, the spectacle will be extended, by elimination of the stage, to the entire hall of the theatre and will scale the walls from the ground up on light catwalks, will physically envelop the spectator and immerse him in a constant bath of light, images, movements and noises. The set will consist of the characters themselves, enlarged to the stature of giant manikins, and of landscapes of moving lights playing on objects and masks . . .

Joan Littlewood (English director of Theatre Workshop)
Tamasha, a Marathi word meaning fun and games, turned out to be pop theatre. It could be played anywhere—village, boulevard or Isle of Wight. The group—tambour, pot, harmonium, drums. The dancing—a girl in a Pola Negri (a silent film star) headdress, Turkish pants with bundles of bells round her ankles: the singer tenor schmaltz. The clowning—the whole ensemble creating street scenes with music and cries, playing encounters, flirtations, intrigues making a shower of crazy cracks while the audience yell back, taking a fifty-fifty share in the fun.

from an article in *The Observer*

Bertolt Brecht (1898–1956)
With what care he (the designer) selects a chair, and with what thought he places it! And it all helps the playing. One chair will have short legs, and the height of the accompanying table will also be calculated, so that whoever eats at it has to take up a quite specific attitude . . .

The master knows every craft and is careful to see that even the poorest furniture is executed in an artistic way, for the symptoms of poverty and cheapness have to be prepared with art. So materials like iron, wood, canvas are expertly handled and properly combined, economically or lavishly as the play demands. He goes to the blacksmith's shop to have the swords forged, and to the artificial florists to get tin wreaths cut and woven. Many of the props are museum pieces.

These small objects which he puts in the actors' hands—weapons, instruments, purses, cutlery,

Joan Littlewood as 'Mother Courage'. Theatre Workshop Festival, 1955.

etc.—are always authentic and will pass the closest inspection: but when it comes to architecture—i.e. when he builds interiors or exteriors— he is content to give indications, poetic and artistic representations of a hut or a locality which do honour as much to his imagination as to his power of observing . . .

In his designs our friend always starts with 'the people themselves' and 'what is happening to or through them'. He provides no 'decor', frames and backgrounds, but constructs space for 'people' to experience something in.

Brecht writing about designer Casper Neher

Reference

Brecht on Theatre trans. J. Willet, Methuen
Theatre and its Double A. Artaud,
  Calder and Boyars
The Stage in Action S. Selden, Owen
Directors on Directing Cole and Chinoy, Owen
Experimental Theatre J. Roose Evans, Studio
  Vista
Effective Theatre J. Russell Brown, Heinemann

Environment

Each activity, project or play will pose the question—is this the right environment? Often the answer will be 'no', and it will have to be changed, by the addition of screens, drawings, photographs, lights, slides, shapes, constructions, sounds, newspaper, card, curtains, blocks or any other method.

In constructing objects and preparing surroundings for drama (including stage settings), the people who are going to be involved must be considered first. What ideas have they? What size are they? How strong are they? What shape are they? Then, what is the nature of the work to be done?

Wood, canvas, plastics, foam rubber, polystyrene, metals, ropes, hessians, scaffolding, packing cases, cardboard cylinders, paper cups, corrugated paper are some aids to changing the environment, apart from mechanical apparatus.

Reference

Planning for Play Lady Allen of Hurtwood,
  Thames and Hudson
Playground and Recreation Spaces Ledermann
  and Trachel, Architectural Press
Kinetic Art G. Brett, Studio Vista

Props

Properties (or 'props') are the objects which are handled. These are visible, and therefore have a visual effect, and should be selected or designed with care. An imaginative approach can be brought to this. Simple objects like broomhandles, chairs, cardboard cut-outs, paper hats, symbolic props, can be highly effective and can encourage an attitude of imaginative freedom.

Reference

Stage Properties and How to Make Them R.
  Kenton, Pitman

Costumes

Costume design has at its centre a human being, who will ask, is the costume comfortable? What does it look like? Physique and shape must be taken into account. Material must be chosen which is comfortable to wear. Material, colour and design should relate to the overall design, to the wearer and to the environment.

For 'free' sessions (games and improvisation), clothing should be comfortable and allow plenty of movement. Shorts, vests, loose fitting slacks will help. Arms free, feet bare.

A collection of hats, masks, oddments of material, scarves, etc. are of great value, especially during improvisation sessions.

Reference

Costume through the Ages J. Laver, Thames and
  Hudson
Drama—its costume and decor J. Laver, Studio
  Vista
Costume in the Theatre J. Laver, Harrap
Costume in Pictures P. Cunnington, Studio Vista
Simple Stage Costume S. Jackson, Studio Vista

Masks and make-up

Both are ancient arts. All the great theatres of the world since classical times have fostered a detailed and intricate form of the language of stylised facial expressions, some invested with a sign-language which takes considerable understanding. Primitive tribes, likewise, have used dynamic masks and stylised expressions with paint for ceremonies and rituals.

Masks are fun to make, and they have tre-

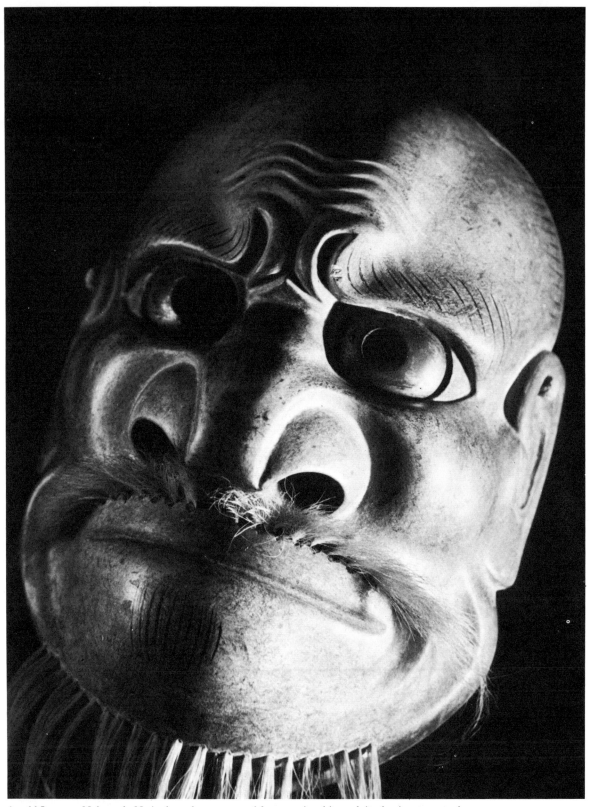

An old Japanese Noh mask. Notice how the exaggerated features give this mask its dominant expression.

10

mendous dramatic potential. They immediately make a statement, and can be the source of the release of dramatic situations. The making of masks can be simple, e.g. out of flat card, or elaborate, e.g. using wire frames, papier mache, rubber solution, or linen with foam rubber built up on it and painted.

Make-up should be used imaginatively, using colour excitingly, and helping the strength of facial expression.

Reference

Tribal Masks E. Herhold, Hamlyn
Primitive Art D. Frazer, Thames and Hudson
Paper Faces M. Grater, Mills and Boon
Practical Stage Make-up P. Perrottet, Studio Vista
The National Portrait Gallery

Light

Light unifies all the elements in drama work. The experience of the whole is totally affected by the condition of light, Natural daylight often gives rise to exciting drama. It allows a person to behave naturally and allows a natural response to colour. A drama space should have access to daylight.

Human beings respond significantly to changes in light, and the creation of effects by artificial lights allows a wide range of different responses. Near-darkness can create worry, suspicion, anticipation, concentration or relaxation. Brilliant light can dazzle and exhaust. Shadows can be menacing, disturbing or distracting, and violent changes in colour can be thrilling or surprising or alarming.

A casual approach to lighting can totally confuse human responses. People may have difficulty in seeing and lose concentration, which often means they then have difficulty in hearing. A flashing beam can distract. A colour can create the wrong atmosphere or emotional response. Artificial light can produce startling effects, which by themselves can be staggering, but which may not relate to the nature of the drama or the people in it.

Stage lighting is subtle and changeable. Small spotlights for a studio area range through to large floodlights for a large acting area. Colour can be added by coloured acetate. (Consult a 'Strand Electric' Colour Chart.)

Electricity throws a strong, steady, sure light. The old 'limelight' was warm, flickering and mellow. Experiments, within the limits of safety, with matches, candles, torches and reflections from metal and foil surfaces would help to underline the variable nature of light, and give improvisation a different and important starting point.

No drama session should be approached without some clear attitude to the available light, and some attempt to regulate it if it appears wrong or inadequate. Actual performances of plays rely heavily on lighting.

Reference

Rank Strand Electric Catalogue (from 29 King Street, London WC2 8JH)
Stage Lighting Frederick Bentham
Stage Lighting B. Fuchs, Blom, NY
Theatrical Lighting Practice Rubin and Watson, Theatre Art Books, NY

b.
Offshoots

Film

Visual effects can be enjoyable to do for their own sakes as experiments and as fun. If they are used in a project, they must be dovetailed in with the other elements of the project. Films are dramatic experiences in their own right. Filmed sequences can also be included in some plays to help the visual interest of the play.

Film is two-dimensional. It is mechanical, and is concerned with relaying an image. People and objects are flattened into two dimensions, which contrasts strongly with life-size three dimensional people moving about in a space. The addition of film into live action creates its own special problems because of size, inflexibility of the image, the difficulty of manoeuvering the apparatus and the flatness of a screen, if one is used. The rigid nature of some shot film must be considered in relationship to the plastic nature of most stage action.

Abstract film, not needing the precision of projection on a screen, creates few problems. Narrative film (or one with a clear and unchangeable image) needs to be regarded as part of the design to succeed. There is, in addition to the three dimensions of people, a flat screen. If used properly, the effect can be exciting.

Some notes on using film in a play :
Film is flat. Plays are three dimensional.
Narrative film needs a white screen. Plays need space.
The narrative film area is static and defined. Plays can move within an area.
The concentration required from an audience on the light of a projected film is quite different from that required by a group of actors. If the two are happening together the relationship between the two must be carefully worked out, otherwise the eye becomes confused and the images blur.

The visual contrast between what is being shown on film and what is happening on stage needs to be carefully looked at from a *dramatic* point of view. Where, for instance, is the screen to be placed in relationship to the actors? What appears on the screen and how does this relate to the actors? The movement of the film itself imposes an interesting contrast to actors. One of the cinema's greatest innovations is that of moving the camera across an object or landscape (i.e. 'panning'). When this is projected it gives the feeling of movement across a static object (the screen). The actor himself, on the other hand, actually moves. The juxtaposition of a moving actor, and a static screen with moving images is a start to exploring the relationship of the two media.

Large mechanically produced pictures can make an exciting environment for the actor. However, it is comparatively easy for the actor to be overpowered by the image.

Projection. 'Front projection' (i.e. the projector placed some way in front of the screen), causes some problems. The beam of light needs to be powerful. Actors and other actions may interfere, although the mixture of actor and image can be interesting.

At times the actors themselves can be used as 'screens'—the images being projected on their clothes. It is interesting to move the screen or screens about. The screens can be varied in shape.

'Back projection' is placing the projector behind the screen. It is more satisfactory, because the picture can appear behind the actors and they do not interfere with the beam of light. A proper back-projection screen is prohibitively expensive, but a sheet of canvas will do. Some types of opaque polythene are very satisfactory and quite cheap. Gauze can also be used.

Certainly the use of moving film is exciting, and can be used with great effect. If the project seems appropriate, and the funds are available (it is quite expensive), it is rewarding.

Reference

Film Making in Schools D. Lowndes, Batsford
Film Making in Schools and Colleges P. Hardcourt and Theobald, British Film Institute

Slides

The static image of a slide creates a totally different impact from that of a moving picture. Slide projectors are more flexible—they are easy to handle and move. The making of slides is much cheaper and more flexible than the handling of a movie film. Effects can be achieved with inks, glues, acetate, grass, hair, egg-shell, etc., etc.

Some suggestions for the use of slides :
Photographs. Reproductions from books, photographs of people or locations. Such photographs can be used to impart information or supply a background to action. A slide can be 'masked off' (areas blacked out), thus varying the shape of the slide. A 'montage' can be built up, that is a succession of pictures which relate to each other and create an overall visual effect. This could make an interesting starting point for a drama. Sound, recorded or live, could be added.
Written words, sentences, messages giving straightforward information or comments on the action.
A series of words, messages, drawings and photographs making a sequence, which leads into, or from, a drama. Impact can be made with the style of the drawing and with the colour.

Effects can be obtained by scratching lettering on black film.

The slides can be totally abstract, either to suggest the location of a scene or to suggest mood. Such slides can be used purely as a stimulus, with action developing out of the ideas suggested.
A series of projectors can be used to project several slides at the same time. This can create interesting effects and can be used with great subtlety and sensitivity. Contrasting pictures and complementary statements can make a complex series of visual backgrounds to drama.

The slide, like the moving film, is a two-dimensional projection. A flat surface will reproduce the slide, but uneven surfaces can be used to break up the flatness. Projections on shapes, angular surfaces, or just people can be useful and interesting.

As with film, the relationship of the image with the living actor needs to be experimented with, because the power of the image can very strongly challenge the effect of the human being.

Reference
Notes on Photo-play A. Francombe, Kodak

Shadows

The idea of 'play with lights' and 'lightshows' is an extension of puppet theatre. This entails the use of a screen and projectors and lights. The shadow play can be related to the idea of shaping the hands to resemble objects or animals in shadow. Puppets, human beings, cut-outs of objects—these can form the basis of the shadow play. Shadows are cast on a screen which tell a story. This can make use of stick puppets, paper cut-outs, buttons, string, cotton, wire, people with masks, indeed anything which when it casts a shadow creates the desired effect. It is an ancient art, but has been re-vitalised by the use of modern materials.

Reference

Play with Light and Shadow Herta Schönewolf, Reinhold/Studio Vista
Puppetry To-day H. Binyon, Studio Vista
Movements in Two Dimensions O. Cook, Hutchinson

The combination of slides, coloured lights, music and recorded voices forms the basis for 'son et lumiere', an entertainment which is built up using purely technical devices. A story is chosen and is told using only technical equipment. The environment is usually pre-arranged, either because it has some connection with the story, or by the creation of scenery.

Should live action be included, it leads towards an idea of 'total theatre'—which is drama involving music, movement, lights, slides, film, dance, song, and anything else that the available talents can contribute.

Sound

Human
Voice : The voice is capable of a variety of sounds. Speaking and singing (which is closely allied to speech; everybody sings when they speak, but not in organised melody). Talking is communicating using language. Language is capable of a wide variety of inflections, accents and variations depending on fashion, location, environment, social class, age, and social movements.

The voice is an instrument; it creates sounds which can be changed, extended, deepened, broadened. Sounds can be experimented with in intensity, volume, pitch, pace, quality (open and

Two young people creating shadow play behind a cotton sheet.

closed). Both the nature of the voice and the nature of the sounds it can make can be explored —speaking rapidly, slowly, imitating others, inventing languages, attempting accents, singing.

The body : Because the body consists of cavities and extensions (arms, legs, hands, feet) and a torso, it can create and aid a whole series of sounds. The abdomen, the chest, the inside of the head, the mouth, nose, throat, can all help to change the nature of sound. Experiment with the projection of sound using different parts of the body as an 'echo chamber'.

Arms and legs, by themselves or with the addition of instruments produce a different kind of sound, not connected with the voice. Hands and feet, by clapping, stamping, rubbing hands together, jumping, kicking, tapping, can increase the range of sound the individual can make.

Instruments

Musical instruments are extensions of the human being. Their use depends upon manipulation by people. They use both the inner resources of the body (wind instruments) and the extensions, mostly the arms and hands. The sophisticated sounds made by musical instruments can be augmented by the use of home-made instruments, such as boxes, tins, sandpaper, blocks of wood, tins of pins, hollow drums, metal tubes, glass jars, etc. The nature of sounds from such things as running water, a typewriter, closing doors, thunder, etc., can be included in sessions devoted to the exploration of sounds.

Such an exploration can form the starting point for an improvisation, extending the effect of various sounds on a group.

Recorded sound

Sound recording has endless possibilities. Sound plays can be made in their own right, developed from a script, and using recorded sounds and voices—the result being like a radio play. Recorded sounds have a large part to play in other

14

drama sessions, both for presentations and informal drama.

The art of recording is mainly one of trial and error, the possibilities become quickly apparent, and the mistakes are very evident. The availability of sounds, as backgrounds and as part of a drama session, is greatly helped by the ability to find the position on a tape-recorder quickly.

Technical drawbacks, such as poor loudspeakers, clicks on the machine, poor recording apparatus, can be overcome simply by not choosing inferior equipment, and when you have good equipment, by not treating it casually.

Records themselves are useful. They can set mood, or provide a stimulus.

Reference

The Tape Recorder in the Classroom J. Weston, Nat. Committee for Visual Aids in Education
Noises Off F. Napier, Garnett Miller
Musical Instruments, made to be played J. Roberts, Dryad Press

Movement

We communicate physically, as well as visually and aurally. Every movement is a statement. Apart from knowing that hands are for picking up, arms for reaching and levering, feet and legs for walking, etc., the manner in which the body is used communicates itself as an expression. We not only look and admire the movement, we react to it.

On a simple level we understand that such things as fear, happiness, menace, illness, timidity, do affect our movement, and other people respond to this. A raised hand is a statement—it could be an irate father, a fascist salute or a question. Everyday movement therefore, has a quality and a language. It announces something about the personality—I am warlike, mild, angry; movement is a 'language'—and there is a language of movement.

Many people are confused by the language. Some assume an artificiality of movement which 'poses' and is untrue. Many of us, forced daily into chairs and desks, forget how to move, and grow tired and inarticulate. We need less to learn how to move, than to re-discover how to move, and to be sure why we are moving.

Games often produce 'good movement' (movement which we recognise as free and pleasant), because they are mostly physical and there is a reason for moving. A drama session started with a game will free the body of fears and tensions, release energies, and clear the mind of nagging problems and worries. Suitable games are suggested in *Dramawork 1*.

Physical exercises will often do much the same sort of thing—stretching parts of the body, rolling up in a ball, running around the room, jumping on to a chair, leaping in the air, rolling around the floor—but because these lack human contact they tend to develop the body only rather than increase the communicability of the movement.

In any case the group will, in some degree, be continually communicating physically. Constantly explore different forms of movement.

Have a session in which no word is spoken. All instructions, methods of communication, must be made through actions.

Create objectives—pick up objects, place them elsewhere—go through 'doors', up 'stairs', into 'rooms', feel the kind of room through movement. Express emotions through movement.

Use the imagination. Imitate the movements of animals (cat, lion, leopard, elephant, etc.). Move on different surfaces (hot, cold, slippery, sharp, sandy, wet, woolly, spikey). Imagine different environments—different weather conditions. Imitate the action of machines.

Explore the movement of people of different age groups and different occupations.

Explore the movement of different parts of the body. Move one foot, move about the floor on the buttocks, crawl about with the chest on the floor, do 'bunny hops', hold the ankles, bend the knees and walk, walk about on the hands, on the hands and feet, do handstands up against a wall.

Group movement. The movement of one person will correspond and juxtapose with that of other members of a group. Observe groups of people—in queues, on street corners, at official gatherings, on the beach, etc.—and attempt to recreate group movements. The group itself will begin to express things together which will lead to group statements, what the group wants to say.

Reference

Improvisation for the Theater Viola Spolin, Northwestern University Press
Towards a Poor Theatre Jerzy Grotowski, Methuen

An Introduction to Kinesiology Marion R. Broer, Prentice-Hall

The Social Matrix of Physical Education Celeste Ulrich, Prentice-Hall

The Silent Language E. T. Hall, Oldbourne Press

Language

Language is the commonest method of communication. Words are a precise method of conveying what we mean. To use words properly, we have to want to convey something. The more difficult the thought, the more we have to learn the language to express it.

We can get away with a few standard words—a verbal shorthand that 'gets us by'. A limited number of movements, a few grunts, several names, an expletive or two and we can exist. However, we can express no thoughts or understand no other minds, without acquiring a vocabulary. Language is the key to the world's drama, and is the key to understanding other people. Language by itself is not drama, which needs action, organisation and visual presentation.

Drama sessions should contain plenty of talk. Discussions, debates and lectures should accompany physical movement. Ideas from books, newspapers, magazines should be brought into the sessions for discussion and argument.

Some word games
The group sits in a circle. First player starts a story. At a certain part of the story he stops, the next player takes over and continues the story. The leader can stop the story-teller. It goes on until the group have finished.

Strike up a rhythm through clapping. Start with any word, and work this into the rhythm. E.g. WORD-clap, clap. Word-clap, clap . . . In a circle, the second player changes the original word to one suggested by the first, e.g. Blue-clap-clap-sky-clap-clap-cloud-clap-clap. Then develop it into a story. I-clap-clap-went-clap-clap-for-clap-clap-a-clap-clap-walk-clap-clap-and-. Vary the rhythm.

Charades. Act out two scenes, each including one syllable of a two-syllable word. Act a third scene containing the whole word.

Divide into four teams. Each team writes a list of words, containing descriptions of people, locations, colours and interesting subjects. The words are all torn off separately, screwed into a ball and put into a hat. Each team takes four pieces of paper and uses the four ideas chosen as the basis for an improvisation.

'Good' and 'bad' language. Standards of language are not absolute. 'Swear' words are sometimes essential to a situation and a necessary part of expression. 'Slang' terms have their place, especially in some environments. Classbound accents can be limiting and alienating. Good language is that which is clear, says what it means and which directly relates the subject matter with the personality of the speaker, using variety, colour, life and interest. Everybody is capable of good speech.

Reference

Communication in Speech A. Wise, Longman
Voice of Poetry in the Conversation of Mankind W. Walsh, Chatto and Windus

Acting

Acting is a highly specialised art. The statement 'everybody can act' needs qualifying. Everybody has it in them to explore and re-act. But 'acting' as a talent can be confused with the capabilities of professional actors, who have learnt a range of attitudes and behaviours which suit them for their profession. A person who is conscious of his ability to create effects can destroy valuable work in drama. Techniques wrongly handled or misunderstood lead to stilted and uncreative drama.

Improvisation is within everybody's range, and is the basis for studio drama work. It is a method of finding the root of drama, the creative tool for exploring a dramatic situation. Language comes to aid the improvisation—the words of the group itself.

Improvisation can be used as a method for development if it is 'evaluated'. At all times part of the group should observe the rest in their improvisation. After it is finished, the whole group should examine the result, questioning what was intended and whether the group succeeded.

This is not to make the work of the group self-conscious, but to suggest that ultimately there are standards that should apply, and that drama is finally directed at communicating with others.

Reference

An Actor Prepares C. Stanislavsky, Penguin
The Messingkauf Dialogues B. Brecht, Methuen

Commedia dell' Arte

a. Introduction

The Commedia dell'Arte was a spirited and vigorous style of entertainment performed by highly skilled professional actors in the sixteenth century. It was a popular art form with comic strip characters who performed in grotesque masks and gaudy costumes and with music. Often, their performances involved daring and perilous acrobatics—it was 'circus with a plot', where action was often more significant than words.

The players did not always rely upon a script, but evolved an effective system where the action sprang from the characters using improvised dialogue. If there was a script the actors reserved the right to treat it with the utmost freedom. The players would often agree upon a plot before the performance. This would be pinned up behind the scenery where the actors would refer to it before making their entrance. Plots were stolen freely from novels, plays, the latest scandal, tavern stories and the like.

As well as a skeletal plot, with only occasionally inserted dialogue, each actor would have a particular character to play. Some actors were said to have played the same character for many years. He would play the same part within a variety of plots, rather like Biffo the Bear, Desperate Dan, Lord Snooty, etc. in the Beano and Dandy comics. Some of the actors would have set speeches and actions which they would adapt to almost any circumstance. Most of the humour was visual with variations on standard jokes thus providing scope for elaboration and improvisation. The whole effect would be gay, colourful and agile with swift-moving action.

The actors would travel from place to place and perform their entertainment in the street, the market place, the fairground, the tavern, often carrying their own portable stage of planks and curtains. The staging was simple, often no more than a crudely drawn street in black lines upon the curtains. Sometimes the curtains would suggest two houses on either side of a street.

Dressed in their costumes, disguised by their masks the actors would enter a town playing a drum, a guitar, a trumpet, singing and dancing around their creaking cart loaded with colourful cloth and a variety of properties used in their plays. The clowns would perform acrobatics giving the populace a hint of what was in the show, like a cinema trailer. The noise would attract the people, some of whom would run out to greet the actors bringing story, a scandal and fun.

Areas of exploration

1. Find out what you can about travelling players and the kind of stages they performed on.
2. Find out about the social conditions of sixteenth century Europe and the kind of life a town dweller had and also the country peasant. Look at pictures by Brueghel.
3. See if you can find pictures of the Commedia dell'Arte characters.
4. How do you think these travelling players were able to keep the attention of noisy, shuffling crowds? What do you think they needed to do?
5. Could you describe a typical day in the life of one of these actors and what you think it might be? (Where do you think they slept? How do you think they eat? What would be the feelings of an actor approaching a town? What would his reaction be to a good crowd/a bad crowd? What would make a good or bad crowd? How would the actor feel after the performance? What would the actors talk about? How would their day end?)

Arlecchino.

b.Some characters

The Commedia characters were generally divided into 'non-comic masks', the serious people, and 'comic masks', the clowns.

The non-comic masks

The Young Lover : His name—Lelio or Flavio or Orazio or Ottavio or Leandro.
His beloved: Her name—Isabella, Flaminia, Lucinda, or Camilla.

Both attractive, usually played without masks and wearing elegant clothes. They were experts in the art of courtship and went through the emotions of young love; sometimes happy, sometimes unhappy, they also scorned one another, hated one another, often despaired, were consoled and also jealous, sometimes parted and at the end returned to each other and married.

The Maids: Names—Spinneta or Nina or Corallina or Columbina.

Usually played without mask, a specialist in quick change disguises. Has a sharp malicious wit, gossipy and gay, sprightly and always willing to help the young lovers. Capricious with man servants whom they sometimes married.

Costume : an ordinary maid's dress.

The Comic masks

Arlecchino (Other names—Arlequin or Harlequin) a servant.

A mixture of stupidity and cunning, he is the chief rascal—a pickpocket. Sometimes lazy and diffident but very agile, he can walk on stilts, do somersaults, can appear as a hunchback without padding and can parody at high speed laughing, bowing, weeping, ridiculous attitudes; generally maintains the rhythm of the comedy. Steals for the fun of it.

Costume : originally a negro in tatters but usually appears in multi-coloured diamond shapes over jacket and trousers. The mask looks like that of a black devil with bushy eyebrows, and moustaches, a snub nose, little holes for eyes. On his belt he carries a purse and a wooden sword.

Brighella a cunning servant.

He is prepared to intrigue, to deceive, to confuse, and is exceedingly resourceful, cynical, and unscrupulous. He enjoys outwitting an old love-sick fool, robbing a miser, beating up a creditor. He guides the comic action by breaking marriages, arranging others, insinuating suspicions, flattering vanity, preparing love potions. He is also adept at other professions: soldier, tavern keeper, hangman, fortune teller, thief.

Costume : a woollen cap, loose shirt, baggy trousers, the colours white and green. His half mask is animal-like with slit eyes and crooked nose, moustaches long and pomaded, a peaked beard. On his belt a purse and a dagger.

Pulcinella has a clucking voice and a habit of imitating chirping chicken; a beak-like nose and a hunched back. Can appear as a servant, a peasant, a dentist, physician, pirate, famous lawyer, painter, simple soldier, retired general, a feigned idiot or a feigned intellectual, superstitious, cowardly, reckless, beater of others and often gets beaten himself; although greedy he can take bread from his own mouth to feed a baby, a chatterbox, never knows when to keep silent or still.

Costume : a mask with a beak nose furrowed with wrinkles, long moustaches, peaked beard, wart or carbuncle on forehead, a sugar loaf hat. A cord at waist and a wooden sword.

The Captain a braggart soldier of fierce appearance, but a coward. He usually has a servant who acts as his squire and encourages his master to recount his formidable exploits. He speaks in a ferocious voice. He struts pompously and talks constantly of terrifying acts of bravery. A vain man who believes he can conquer woman with overplayed gallantry and ceremony, he looks ridiculous.

Costume : sometimes shabby, sometimes elegant, a huge feathered hat, large riding boots, a long sword and a scarlet cloak. His mask is set in a ferocious leer, a long hooked nose, fierce moustaches.

Sometimes has a name: Spavento, Scarramonti, Terremoto, Matamoros and speaks with a strong Spanish accent.

Pantalone sometimes father/husband/widower/old bachelor. Sometimes poor/rich/miserly. Sometimes bankrupt/rich noble.

Avaricious, lover of pomp and splendour, wily yet rash, slanderous, quarrelsome, subject to sudden explosions of fury and vehement outbursts of curses. Lustful—unseemly for one of his years. His voice is harsh, laugh strident, moves in a hunched manner, when angry is capable of incredible feats of agility which leaves him in a state of exhaustion panting asthmatically. Occasional ridiculous backfalls when he receives a startling piece of bad news or revelation.

Costume : predominantly red, long tight breeches, a black robe lined with red. The half mask is of a bony face, hooked nose, bushy eyebrows, long white moustaches and white hair, pointed beard. At his belt he wears a purse and also a dagger. He wears yellow slippers.

The Doctor in his sixties, a lawyer or physician; sometimes a father. Friend and rival of Pantalone.

The doctor is usually eager for a romantic adventure, but ends up the object of derision. A busy-body, a muddler, presumptious, his tirades are incomprehensible with words mispronounced and Latin and Greek misquoted. Other characters often labour in vain to interrupt him. He is obese, loquacious, and a glutton. A caricatured professor. He is clumsily dignified, manner highly stylised, sways as he walks mincing in tiny steps. Often holds a book, gesticulates professorially with index finger.

Costume : completely black except for wide white collar, cuffs and handkerchief that hangs from his belt. The half mask has a bulbous nose, flaccid cheeks, huge red wart, black moustaches.

Pantalone.

Two Commedia characters which could form the basis of costume designs for a Commedia style show.

Coviello.

21

Coviello : a shrewd and adroit servant, supple and vain, often threatens invisible enemies with a wooden sword, repeats everything said by his master, if not word for word, idea for idea.

Costume : ridiculous, huge buttons running the whole length of his body, his hat is heavily plumed. His mask has a long nose, bright red cheeks and a black brow.

Tartaglia : the stutterer, a gossiping servant, often unable to complete the articulation of words and therefore often flies into a rage with frustration with himself and with others. Often professes to be brave but will hide himself if hearing a cock crow. He fills a number of roles: notary, policeman, advocate, judge, apothecary—invariably ridiculous.

Costume : enormous linen coloured coat, pantaloons traversely striped with green and yellow, white stockings and black shoes. He is either very fat or very thin. His mask has a prominent nose, is beardless and he wears an enormous pair of blue spectacles.

The Constable : often played by Arlecchino.

A vast felt hat, strongboots, long sword, enormous moustachios and a large nose. This outfit would hang upon a nail behind the scenes and the whole put on like a dressing gown by the servant who would play constable.

But often there would appear on the other side of the stage a real constable who moves in the shadow wrapped to the eyes in his cloak—but his heavy boots make so much noise that only the deaf would not hear him.

C. Exercises

Exploration

Try some of the characteristics of the characters, either each in turn or choose a character you would like to play and try the following exercises.

(i) Read one of the character outlines about a Non-comic or Comic Mask.

(ii) Make a mask for the character you have chosen.

(iii) Once you have made the mask, look in a mirror and begin to take on the attitude of the character. Invent a way of walking and later invent a voice for the character.

(iv) Find a partner and invent a dialogue in character where one partner tries to persuade the other to get money by either fair means or foul.

(v) The partner returns and has to explain in detail how he/she got, or didn't get the money.

(vi) Each partner to have a rolled length of newspaper.
(a) In pairs to play club tag.
(b) One character chases another for betraying him.

In pairs and in character

Arlecchino and Brighella : Brighella tells us that he is plotting to make a fool of Pantalone, who he knows is in love with Isabella and that he has managed to persuade Pantalone that Isabella will marry him. Brighella has acted as messenger, and, according to Brighella, today is the day of the wedding and Pantalone has promised to reward Brighella when Isabella appears at the church in a wedding gown. When Arlecchino appears

Brighella, after much arguing and persuasion, gets Arlecchino to dress up as Isabella.

Isabella and Flavio : strike attitudes of happy love, then sadness, followed by:

>   scorn
>   hate
>   despair
>   jealousy
>   consolation
>   marriage

Strike the attitude and state its word.
Invent sentences or phrases while striking the attitude.
Invent conversations so that we know why they are happy, sad, scornful, hateful, jealous, consoled and why they agree to marry.

Pantalone and the Doctor : Pantelone tries to convince the Doctor that he is the right man for Isabella by telling him that he still has a fine figure, is able to run and jump, and will make Isabella the happiest woman in the world. The Doctor laughs, he wants Isabella as well, and he too tells Pantalone how fit a man he is for Isabella. This makes Pantalone exceedingly angry, he throws a violent temper which is so active he ends up on the floor panting.

The Captain and Pulcinella : The Captain tells us about his exploits at the war in which he was the bravest of fellows. He demonstrates how he, single handed fought a whole battalion. They were fierce and unruly and how he rescued a beautiful princess from their villainous clutches. While he tells this story, Pulcinella encourages him and behind his back mimics him, indicating that what the Captain is saying is completely untrue.

And now the Captain has returned from the wars to claim the love of his childhood dreams— Isabella.

From those four scenes it is possible to write the plot of a Commedia style play; adding meetings between other characters. Write an outline scene for:

>   Brighella and Isabella
>   Pantalone and the Captain
>   The Doctor and Harlequin
>   Pulcinella and Arlecchino
>   Pantalone and Brighella
>   Columbina and all Isabella's visitors

The basic idea being that all the men except the servants want to marry Isabella, and Isabella finally decides she wishes to marry Flavio. The servants conspire and trick to keep the other men away from Isabella, while the men try to keep each other away through the deployment of their servants—who never quite do what they're told.

Although there are many elaborations the basic plot of a Commedia dell'Arte play was generally about youth versus age, with two young people in love in the centre of the action, while parents, guardians and rivals employed all kinds of devices to prevent the lovers meeting and the servants used complicated stratagem to help the lovers.

Reference

The Commedia dell'Arte Giacomo Oreglia, Methuen

The History of the Harlequinade Maurice Sand, Blomm

A Concise History of the Theatre Phyllis Hartnoll, Thames and Hudson

The History of Harlequin Cyril W. Beaumaont, Blomm

The Seven Ages of Theatre Richard Southern, Faber

The World of Harlequin A. Nicoll, Cambridge

d.Extensions & Ideas

Invent your own clown

Experiment in making a clown's nose: long, bulbous, or crooked; and/or make a moustache: short, waxed or flowing; or make a long beard (from your chin to your feet)

Experiment in the use of stage make-up; paint your face blue, red, black, yellow, white or use a variety of shapes on your face similar to that of a circus clown.

Experiment with various kinds of footwear: slippers, large boots, bandaged feet, wear short wooden 'planks' tied to your feet so that you clack as you walk or bare feet (especially if you are an acrobatic clown)

Experiment with wearing ill-fitting clothes: shoes too big, vast and baggy trousers, tight trousers where the trouser legs reach only to the calf, a jacket where the sleeves hang over the hands, or work up to the elbow, coat tails that trail along the floor. Try wearing a variety of clothes, especially clothes that have a dominant characteristic which in turn will suggest a character for your clown: drab sackcloth or elegant clothes, rich in colour, a coat with large buttons or clothes tied up with string. Find a hat: large or small, decorated with streamers or feathers or not at all.

Experiment in the use of a property: a cane, an umbrella, a sunshade, a stick with bells on, balloons, a water pistol, a pop gun, a stick with a soaked sponge on the end, a metal bath on wheels, a cloak.

Study each clown then experiment by drawing and painting different clown faces. Then paint your own face.

24

In pairs

Find a partner, ride on his shoulders, wrap yourselves in a large piece of cloth and be a very tall woman.

Find a partner who is your opposite: fat/thin, drab/gay, slow/quick, tall/short.

Invent a mock bull-fight.

Play ball, jugglers, knife throwers, sword dancers, thief and policeman with imaginary properties.

Play musical instruments: a kazzoo, a tambourine, spoons, castanets, drum, comb and paper, 'jew's' harp, mouth organ. Invent a musical double act and dance routine.

Play the Yes/No game. One of the partners continually asks questions of the other who must answer honestly without saying yes or no.

Invent a 'Laurel and Hardy' act. Whatever one does to the other the other replies similarly. Each act being more outrageous than the previous one. Not a single word is spoken.
    A tie is flicked out of place.
    A handkerchief is snatched from the pocket.
    A hat is knocked off the head.
    The hat is stamped on.
    As the owner of the hat bends over to pick it up, the other kicks him and sends him onto his face.
The performance is carried out in silence without so much as a flicker of expression. In the face of impending disaster neither must flinch or do anything at all. In such an act, the clown sees the pie coming, and with eyes open waits for the inevitable. No attempt is made to evade it.

With your partner find and act 'I say, I say' gags.
1st Clown: I say, I say, I say, my wife's gone to
        the West Indies.
2nd Clown: Jamaica?
1st Clown: No, she went of her own accord . . .

Invent gags of your own. On the other hand you might discover jokes and humorous inventions in the *Lore and Language of Schoolchildren* by I. and P. Opie which will provide starting points for comic material which you can translate into material for clowns. See chapters: *Just for Fun, Wit and Repartee, Guile, Riddles, Parody and Impropriety,* etc.

In groups of four, five, six or seven, elaborate and act the following points. Be inventive and remember that clowns need to be committed to what they are doing. They believe, no matter how outrageous or illogical the action, that the problem is real.

Scene: Paris, seventeenth century

A miser and his son are rivals for the hand of a beautiful young lady. The son gets possession of a casket containing the miser's treasure. He gives his father the choice between the young lady and the casket. The loss of the casket reduces the miser to frenzy. The old man chooses the casket and abandons the young lady to his son.

(from *The Miser* by Moliere)

Scene: Venice, seventeenth century

A rich merchant, without children pretends to be dying in order to draw gifts from would-be heirs. His servant and co-plotter persuades each of these in turn that he is to be the heir and thus extracts costly presents from them. One even sacrifices his wife to the merchant in hope of the inheritance. To enjoy the discomfigure of the would-be heirs the merchant pretends to die after making everything over to his servant. The servant takes advantage of his position and tries to blackmail the merchant, his master. A lawyer, who had sacrificed his wife, reveals the whole matter in court to the judges. Whereupon he, and the merchant and the servant are punished, their wealth confiscated by the state.

(from *Volpone* by Ben Jonson)

Scene: Athens, 4th century B.C.

A rich merchant has left for a voyage, leaving his son to look after his house. The son turns the house into a palace of pleasure and incurs many debts. During a party the father returns, but the son's servant is able to persuade the father that the sound he hears is that of ghosts and that the son has deserted the house and bought the one the other side of the square, which in fact is occupied by people now on holiday . . .

(from *The Ghost* by Plautus)

Laurel and Hardy in 'The Blockheads'. Note the contrast in their size and facial expression.

The Clown's Carnival

This is a short actable clown show. Work on the character scenes first: the two Pulcinellas and their wife, the Captain and the servant, the Doctor, the servant and the two fools; then work on the crowd scenes: the entry of the crowd, the girl's dance, the creation of the spectre and its disintegration, the crowning of Pulcinella and the final procession. You may find it more workable to have a separate orchestra.

The characters :

Two Pulcinellas	Two Fools
Wife to Pulcinella	The Captain
Arlecchino	Pantalone
The Doctor	A Servant

A crowd of clowns (some can be the spectre) both male and female.

Scene: An empty street

The sound of a trumpet. A moment later, Pulcinella enters playing. He stops and looks round.

Pulcinella: Behold! Here I am Pulcinella, playing a trumpet and there's no one here, except you. Listen. *Silence*
Not a sound. No one. They're all lazy. It passes the twentieth hour and they're not ready yet! I'll go and beat them up. Don't go away.

He runs off. Silence . . . Arlecchino, on tiptoe, leading a crowd of people all silent. Arlecchino carries a lantern, leading a man and a woman by the hand. They are followed by a clown carrying an umbrella.

Arlecchino: Look how the moon and the sun shines both at the same time. Sunshade and lantern. Night and morning.

Suddenly there is a great noise and the whole crowd begin to dance. Two identical Pulcinellas, each chasing the same girl who is dressed as a female Pulcinella—obviously a wife—but of which one? Neither of the Pulcinellas is sure, neither is she, so they alternately kiss and scorn one another.

A group of girls, their faces covered with white masks, their long hair falling to their shoulders and dressed entirely in white, perform a gay and simple dance to the rhythm of tambourines.

The Captain storms into the scene, arguing and shouting, chasing a servant and brandishing his sword. The crowd freeze.

Captain: If you don't return at once to the galleys I will cut you in two, piece of a thief.

He raises his sword over the cowering servant who screams.

Suddenly there enters a group of fools, dressed in long white shirts, wearing night-caps and white masks, necks smothered in enormous ruffs, carrying tambourines, performing acrobatics, some armed with sticks from the end of which hangs a wet sponge. And as the Captain is about to bring his sword across the poor servant's neck the servant screams: 'You make a mistake . . . I'm not the one you're looking for.'

The Captain is lifted up struggling, while the servant dashes off into the crowd. Noise and the dance continues.

The noise stops and the crowd freeze.

The Doctor enters with a book under his arm. The fools have caught the servant again, who is again placed in a humiliating position of being on his knees. The servant is not masked.

Doctor *standing over the servant*: You are my debtor, these last two years, these last two centuries. At last I've found you. Your grandfather, your great-great grandfather, your devil of an ancestor wrote me a bill of exchange. You don't believe it? Do you deny it? I will show it to you.

The Doctor opens the book, which is a box full of flour, he blows into it, sending the flour into the servant's face who was gaping at him. The Doctor goes into the crowd. A fool dusts the servant down. Another sweeps him.

Volpone, National Theatre. Note the use of false noses, heavy eyebrows, and beards which help to emphasize the characterization.

Fool 1: My you have gone pale.
Fool 2: He is about to die . . .

And with that they lift him up and carry him off.

Noise and the dance continues . . . The noise stops and the crowd freeze. A strange, eerie sound fills the street. The people look apprehensively at one another. Whispers: 'What's that noise? What's happening?' Shouts: 'A spectre!'

The figures of Pulcinella, Arlecchino, Brighella, Pantalone cut a thousand different capers of terror, The Captain draws his sword—and hides. And to this strange noise figures dressed in white from head to foot grow into a great white shape that moves and then disintegrates to great shouts as Pulcinella comes forward with giant wooden sword slowly flailing in all directions.

Shouts: The King, the King.

Two fools make a horse, a girl comes forward and crowns Pulcinella with flowers. There is a great jubilant noise of kazoos, drums, tambourines, rattles, trumpet as the King rides the backs of the fools, processing around the area before disappearing down the street.

Again the street is empty. Silence falls.

Documentary

a. Work
b. It's a good life...
c. The Navigators
d. The Voyage of
   the Lucky
   Dragon

a. Work *

Cinema, television, national newspaper, and radio have all risen to prominence and influence in the twentieth century. The effect of these has been to circulate much more quickly and freely, ideas, information, news, fashions and personalities. They have all become part of, and added to, our expectations of entertainment, and much of the drama we experience, outside our everyday lives, comes to us through these media.

Films, plays, musicals, songs, pop music, current events, tend to get merged into an experience of continuous electronic sights and sounds, and real life happenings are increasingly accessible through the camera and the microphone. While on the one hand we have to adjust and not live in a constant fantasy of pictures, on the other we have more easily available a greater insight into the world around us.

It is understandable that the techniques of TV and cinema should find their way into plays, and that the subjects treated by the camera should be explored in drama. There have been a number of notable explorations into the realms of reality in the theatre, ('The Theatre of Fact' or Documentary Theatre), such as 'Oh What a Lovely War' at Theatre Workshop in London, and 'The Knotty' in Stoke-on-Trent.

The 'creative treatment of actuality' is a well-tried method for a group to develop a series of ideas. Any subject from the world around can be approached, from the life cycle of an animal to the history of a local football club.

Each subject will produce a vast amount of material which must be sifted, selected and organised. The whole group can be concerned in the collection of material. The history of the football club, for instance, will produce information about exciting games, personality problems, extraordinary players, money troubles, management drama, success and failure stories. The material will reflect the moods of the periods being looked at.

Such material has to be translated into drama, using dramatic techniques and skills. Songs, sketches, dramatisations of incidents, etc., etc., using masks, films, slides, musical material, newspaper headlines, costume, make-up, movement, lighting . . . moulded into an entertainment which has a point of view and which the group is interested in.

The excerpt that follows is from a documentary study made by a group of young people about young people. It was in various parts. This one is about 'Work'. The technique adopted was:

(a) to read as much as possible on the subject
(b) to go out into the locations and meet people, observe the locality, and ask questions
(c) to use the young people's own experiences.

The material was collected together and sorted into a shape, adding quotations from different sources. Pictures and music were used to expand the ideas already selected.

This episode should be regarded as a starting point—a guide as to how material was assembled and one way of looking at the dramatisation of a documentary subject.

The extract is divided into sections and is followed by notes which comment how the unit was put together.

A *Acting area.* Industrial appearance. Scaffolding. Screens at each side. Pictures of factories and work environments on the screens. A large group of young people sit around. They put on caps, scarves, hats, etc., representing working clothes.

B *Some of them, acting as parents, comment :*
1. I'd like him to take up chemistry. It's completely unproductive and therefore well paid.
2. I want the boy to become a doctor or a farmer. Not to work in a factory or be a porter like me.
3. I don't want him to be in manual work. I'd sooner he worked with his brains than his hands.
4. Business managers. They're not doing anything. They get their money for walking around.

* From *Events leading to a situation from which people find themselves unable to escape.*

5. Civil Servants—I could find other ways of using my money.

6. Agricultural labourers: you can't do without grub.

7. Coal miners—without coal, industry stops.

8. Bricklayers—you've got to have food, and after that houses.

C *A hooter sounds.* The whole group move together, and stand huddled, as if outside the factory gates. They chatter and chunter, making an uneven mumbling sound. They stop.

D *One youth steps forward :* I aim to be something more than a cog in a routine machine. I'm 16½ and I work on tugs. I don't like it much, but I'm not going to work in a factory. That's all there is around here, factories. But what can I do? I can't read or write. What's life anyway? You go to school at five, you leave at 15, get a job, leave at 65 and then die. That's life. What is it that teenagers are supposed to do?

E *The factory hooter sounds again,* and the chuntering people huddle and walk as through

'People walk through the factory gate.'

'People carry on at their various jobs.'

factory gates. They spread out through the acting area and mime a variety of routine jobs. As they work they sing.

F *Reaction*

> *I'm heading straight for something*
> *And I don't know what it is.*
> *It's something I'm not sure of*
> *But I know it's something big.*
>
> *Something big*
> *Is pushing me around.*
> *I know that.*
> *It kicks me when I'm down*
> *In some sort of hopelessness.*
> *I know I must react*
> *In some sort of hopelessness.*
> *I know I must react*
> REACTION

> *This unknown force keeps coming*
> *And I don't know what it is.*
> *It's something I can't cope with*
> *And I know it's something big.*
>
> *A tidal wave is breaking over me.*
> *I know that.*
> *I'm driftwood in its way.*
> *In some sort of hopelessness*
> *I know I must react.*
> *In some sort of hopelessness.*
> *I know I must react.*
> I NEED DIRECTION. I NEED DIRECTION.
> I NEED DIRECTION.

G When the song has finished, the people carry on at their various jobs. Three actors detach themselves and form themselves into an interviewing board.

H *A girl goes to be interviewed.*

Man: Now Miss O'Connor. This is Mr. Fowler, the Manager, and Miss Smythe, the Personnel Manager.

Girl: Oh. Howdy'do.

The interview freezes. The workers are still miming at the factory.

One worker: Portering's a family game. My father has been a meat porter for more than fifty years. You grow up to it. That's where my family is.

Back to the interview.

Mr. Fowler: What makes you want to be a punchcard operator Miss O'Connor? Have you any qualifications?

Girl: No. I haven't got no exams. My friend's a punchcard operator, and I always wanted to be.

Another worker: I am going to try and make my son a waterman—it's a skilled trade. I've applied to the Union Branch, and with any luck he will be taken on as an apprentice when he is fifteen, and by the time he is twenty he will have a good trade on his hands.

Mr. Fowler: Well, thank you Miss O'Connor. We'll let you know.

The Girl goes.

Mr. Fowler: No chance at all I'm afraid.

Miss Smythe: Completely unsuitable.

Another worker: My uncle is well to do. He owns an ice cream business, but he won't give any help to our Gran or us. His wife is stuck up. Her father is a sales manager for some big firm, and she thinks she's better than Princess Margaret, and she won't even set a foot in the East End.

I *A hooter goes.* The people stop work. Throughout the above, the mime has continued. The people go back through the gates and disperse.

J More pictures on the screens of work situations, followed by leisure time activities such as clubs, pubs, youth clubs, etc.

K *Two boys and two girls meet.*

1st boy: I've chucked up my job.

1st girl: Again?

1st boy: Yeah, well only for a few weeks.

2nd boy: What yer going to do?

1st boy: Dunno. Don't care. It's like being on holiday.

2nd girl: Yeh, but what job are you gonna get? What yer gonna do?

1st boy: What can you do? There's nothing.

Voices from young people sitting around the edges.

Voice: Boring.

2: Hanging around.

2nd girl: Let's go down the Wimpy.

2nd boy: What can we do down there—they charge you just for sitting there at this time of night.

Silence.

2nd girl: Let's go up West.

1st girl: Oh no. I don't like it up there. It's too late for the pictures.

1st boy: Oh let's just hang around again.

Stillness.

2nd boy has disappeared. Nothing happens. 2nd boy comes running in with a bicycle.

2nd boy: Hee, hee, look what I've found.

'Sitting around.'

The others rush up and start to inspect the stolen bicycle. As they are looking at it very excitedly, they point out its good features. They freeze, bending over the bike. One of the young people at the side says :

L Just for laughs. That's all we do it for. We take a few things, but nothing much. Bikes—we must have stolen hundreds of the things. People just leave them lying about. I did it with Lennie and the boys. When you'd ridden them around for a bit, I dumped them in the canal, or sold them in the lane. Just walk up and down the lane with a bike, and somebody'll give you a couple of quid for it.

Another voice: Sometimes we go joyriding, there's nothing else to do around here.

M *The group standing round the bike breaks.*

1st boy: How much money you got?
2nd boy: Not much. How about you?
1st boy: A couple of bob.
1st girl: What about getting some?
1st boy: O.K.
1st girl: 'Ere what about that cigarette machine over there on the wall. They hold about ten quid them things.

The two boys go over and try to break it open.

1st girl: Pull it off the wall.

The two boys mime pulling the machine off the wall. They succeed. It is very heavy. The 2nd girl runs across with the bike. They put the 'machine' on the bike with difficulty and run off, steadying the bike.

N *One of the boys at the side :*
I'm going for the money now, I'm ten quid in debt. We're off doing things for a laugh now. Last laugh I had cost me twelve weeks.
Another: And I lost my job; my eighth.
Another: It's boredom mostly—there's nothing to do around here. You get this sort of compulsion, and once you've got that, you'll do anything.

O *The factory hooter sounds.* People re-assemble for work. They mumble and chatter. The hooter goes again, and they go through the 'gates'. Inside they divide into two groups. One is the management, the other the workers. Between them stands the 16½ year-old boy who spoke at the beginning.

The two groups confront each other :
They chant :

Managers: Do this. Do this. Do this. Do this. Do this. Do this. Do th-th-th-this.
Workers: Do what. Do what. Do what. Do what. Do what. Do-what. Do wha-wha-wha-what.
Managers: Do that. Do that. Do that. Do that. Do that. Do that. Do th-th-th-that. Do this. Do that. Do this. Do that. Do this. Do tha-tha-tha-that.
Workers: Who me. Who me. Who me. Who me. Who me. Who me. Who m-m-m-me. Who me.
Managers: Yes you. Yes you. Yes you. Yes you. Yes you. Yes you. Yes y-y-y-you. And you. And you, And you. And you. And you. And you. And y-y-y-you.
Workers: All right. All right. All right. All right. All right. All right. All r-r-r-right.

P *Boy in centre :* It's impossible. There is no way out of this situation. People will say we're going wrong, that we should be flogged. People will say we're criminal. Perhaps we are. But why are we? In spite of my wages which sound quite good, I don't earn much. Not as much as many others do. And I won't get anywhere much. That talk about 'getting on' is moonshine. In the end I'll settle down and be quite happy. But I'll never get to the position of you lot—never, unless I rob a bank or a train or something. Anyway, around here everybody steals. Mums and dads too. For us it's natural—the way we see it, it's simply them and us. Their schools are boring, their work is boring, their clubs and evening classes are boring. How many of our schools are there or clubs or evening classes? How many magistrates sons have ever been in the position of needing to pinch a cigarette machine?

Q *Four Actors stand away from the two groups.*
1. Somebody's got to do boring jobs.
2. They make me sick. Why don't they stop complaining and just get on with it?
3. The streets of our urban slums are slowly filling with young men who have no prospect of finding manhood through work.
4. Alienate them from technology and the price will be high. Bigger and better youth clubs will not work. Neither will bigger and better borstals.

The hooter goes. People break from their groups. They go out through the 'gates'.

Notes

The initial idea stemmed from hearing about the experiences of some young people in a magistrate's court. The group concerned spoke to these young people and the magistrates. They discovered a series of conflicts which had occurred at home, at school, in the streets and at work. Discussions, meetings and books gave a mass of facts which were divided into sections, such as 'Home', 'School', 'Work'.

A Acting area. An open space, with suggestions of an industrial area. It had to be general and suffice in the representation of schools, homes, borstals, etc. Those taking part had to take on roles as parents, teachers, workers, etc. so they wore a basic outfit and added hats, scarves, overalls, etc. (in the style of Commedia dell'Arte actors). Some of the group had taken photographs, and these were used where applicable on slides.

B These were quotations from actual parents, and from *Family and Kinship in East London* by Michael Young and Peter Willmott (Pelican).

C To give dramatic form to the scene it was built around the idea of people going to work in a factory. Although they all do different jobs they start as a group together and respond to the hooter.

D A quotation from a $16\frac{1}{2}$ year-old boy. It was put here because it summed up a statement about work expressing the attitude of the young workers, and was thought to be relevant to the point of the scene.

E We see them doing routine jobs. They repeat actions and then yawn and then repeat actions, as a mime. It is very repetitive. A whole range of jobs was explored: typing, lifting packing cases, licking stamps, stacking books, operating a lathe, making chocolates, storing bread, etc., etc. Each member of the group found an action which represented the job and continued with the action throughout the scene.

F Song written independently by one of the group. The writer (Gordon Tait) imagined it to be sung by a 14 year-old boy who knew there was a great force of opposition bearing down upon him. It was put in this position because it seemed to express the frustration and irony of the situation. It can be spoken.

G The actions carry on through the song. The interview that follows takes place physically in the centre of the actions, which continue. The girl tries to get a job outside the factory. This short scene developed out of improvisation and because those doing it identified very strongly with it, it always had great vitality.

H The quotations, which come from the people who still carry on with their actions, come from *Family and Kinship in East London*. The idea was to build up a composite picture of an interview (and the management), the workers working, and a series of actual statements. The statements were chosen first, the action grew around them.

I The hooter draws the group together again.

J More use of relevant slides.

K This scene was based on discussions with boys and girls in a youth club.

L A quotation from a paper on delinquency collected by one of the group.

M A development of the youth club discussion. The scene was a result of a later improvisation.

N Various quotations from different young people. Each member of the group kept a notebook in which he kept notes and observations. These were in constant use as reference and quotations were often made from these notes in the script.

O A group chant with an insistant beat. A drum or instrumental accompaniment.

P This was a speech composed for the play. It pulled together themes that had been expressed up to that moment, used ideas of the group to express their point of view of the situation they had discovered while researching.

Q These quotations and statements widely represented views of adults and were put in to contrast with the views of the boy.

times—and where these seem to have been reflected in his books. The later part of the exploration included dramatisations of three short stories (not given here)—*The Bike, To Be Collected* and *Revenge*.

(N.B. A useful reference is *The Times Authors—4. Alan Sillitoe*—a folder containing relevant papers, pictures and quotations.)

This is an exploration on three counts:
(i) A delving into the writings of Alan Sillitoe, an English novelist born in 1928.
(ii) A look at the social history of this country during the 'thirties' and 'forties'.
(iii) The use of technical aids, such as slides, tape-recordings, sounds, music and film.

The outline given here is a sketch. It takes the idea of a person born in 1928 and by (a) reading his books, (b) looking at historical records, (c) using recorded material of the time, together with what photographs and films can be obtained, traces through some ideas suggested by events. There are countless ways of working on such an idea. Some that may be interesting are:

1. Trace a social history of Great Britain from 1928 to the present day. Fill in a time chart with key happenings. What are the predominant features of everyday life? What are the key fashions, films, plays, advertisements, sports of the time? Follow fashions, find old magazines. Collect old records, pictures of old film stars. Talk to people who have lived through the time. Collect their anecdotes.

2. Read some of the stories from the collection *The Loneliness of the Long-Distance Runner* by Alan Sillitoe. Especially interesting is *The Decline and Fall of Frankie Buller*. Look at sections in the early part of *Key to the Door*, and from the collection *The Ragman's Daughter*, the short story called *The Bike* is very applicable for dramatisation at the end of the ideas given here.

3. The use of slides and other material. In this case the visual and technical material is put forward as part of the development of the period in question. It would be interesting to attempt to reproduce the styles of the various times in question, thus creating an evolution of ideas, fashions and media which in some way creates the superficial front behind which real events took place.

On the other hand, all the suggested ideas for

b. It's a good life...

Exploring authors

The lives of authors, scientists, explorers, politicians, and monarchs, have often formed the basis for plays. Similarly novels and stories by various authors have made a fertile hunting ground for material for drama. Often a full-scale play can evolve from a novel, such as *Oliver Twist* or *Lord of the Flies*, and the short story can be a fruitful source for a dramatisation, or a poem or a paragraph may suggest a theme for an improvisation.

Authors often return to themes which interest or obsess them, and a thread can be traced in several books, often the attitudes and language used have a common root. A shadowy idea of the author himself sometimes emerges from his writing. Improvisation around selected themes from an author's work can give an idea of his reaction to the times he lives in, and as such prove an interesting counterbalance to factual history. The combination of historical and biographical detail, documentary evidence, such as photographs, drawings and maps, and passages from the writings of a particular author offers a fascinating glimpse into literature and dramatic exploration, extending the idea of straightforward dramatisation.

Such an approach would be interesting with most writers; Charles Dickens, Herman Melville, H. G. Wells, D. H. Lawrence, George Orwell, Ernest Hemingway, Albert Camus, Thomas Hardy, James Joyce are some that suggest themselves. The following is part of such an exploration of the writings of Alan Sillitoe. The piece started with the reading of many of his books, ear-marking passages, finding out facts about the slides and lights can be done easily in other ways:

Instead of slides:
  (i) People with placards giving the information
  (ii) An announcer
  (iii) A loudspeaker

Instead of lights:

A complicated lighting plot isn't strictly necessary. It could be done with (a) a simple series of isolated spotlights or (b) variations of a straightforward general light.

Setting:

The whole piece can be improvised, using desks, boxes, wooden struts, etc.

Alan Sillitoe was born in 1928. He was brought up in Nottingham, and went to school there. When he was 14 he started work at 'the Raleigh', the bicycle factory. At 18 he joined the RAF. He published his first novel, *Saturday Night and Sunday Morning* in 1958. This is part of a series of improvisations suggested by some of his writings, and using some of the facts about his early life.

First improvisation

Acting space. A table. Piled with books. People enter the acting space as if to a library. Each one selects a book from the pile. Each one suggests a character. They stand around reading. The librarian sits behind the table.

Librarian: Now let me see, what was it I had to do? What was the name of that author I had to order. Sillitoe, that was it, Alan Sillitoe. What's it say here?

The other characters all stop their reading and crane forward.

Librarian: He has published ten books in the last ten years. Early books include, *The Loneliness of the Long-Distance Runner* and *Saturday Night and Sunday Morning*. When he was 18 he did his national service. He left school when he was 14 and went to work in a bicycle factory. He was eleven when the war broke out, and he was evacuated. When he was eight there was war in Spain. When he was a baby his father was on the dole. He was born in 1928.

During this recital, the other characters have been moving around the librarian. On the last line they build a sound like a time-machine together, and suddenly throw the books away.

Second improvisation

A screen at the back of the area shows the date 1928. A piano plays 'silent film music'. A decorated sign, 'Welcome to the Roxy Cinema'. Lights flicker. Two characters, dressed as Laurel and Hardy appear in the flickering light. On the screen a part of a film of the time could be shown, Eisenstein's 'October', Hitchcock's 'Blackmail' or a Laurel and Hardy short or other silent comedians. People wearing approximations of 'twenty's' clothes walk through the acting area, sit on seats provided. The piano gives way to a record of the time, a jaunty bouncing tune. The lights come up, pink and rosy. People sit in rows. A red-nosed comedian is just finishing his act:

Red-nosed comedian: My wife's gone to the West Indies.
Voice: Jamaica?
Red-nosed comedian: No. She went of her own accord. Thank you very much ladies and gentlemen.

There is applause. The comedian goes off, and the cinema manager, in smart suit and smart hair-cut appears.

Manager: Thank you, thank you. Well, ladies and gentlemen, I hope you enjoyed the show. This is just a sample of the entertainment you can expect at the new Roxy. Films, music, and fun. I hope you'll come next week, to see 'Show People' starring Marion Davies.

More applause. The ice-cream sales girl walks through the crowd.

'Ice cream, chocolates.'

The people file out. They go out into the streets. Picture on screen: Sordid back-streets. Poverty. There is a succession of pictures, either photographs or drawings. A tinny tune plays on an old fashioned gramophone. The colours change from pink and rosy to dim and dingy. People shuffle through the darkness. One part of the acting area becomes a house. A family sitting around. The father is sleeping.

Third improvisation (based on parts of *Key To The Door*).

Mother: Look at him. Lazy beggar. Hasn't done a stroke of work. Worn out from getting his dole money. I've a good mind to help meself to a few bob. Go down the pub for a bit. Don't get much entertainment around here.

She creeps up to him, puts her hand gently in his pocket, and takes out a note.

Mother: Good. There we are.
She leaves the 'house area'. People walking about. 'Evening Missis.' There is a pause for a moment. Sounds of the neighbourhood. Music again. The mother returns drinking from a jug. She goes into the house area singing; 'I want to be happy'. The father stirs. He feels in his pocket. Turns on the mother.

Father: I've told you before about going down my pockets.
Mother: It's all right, love.
Father: It's not all right. *He hits her viciously.*
Mother *sprawled out:* You pig. We don't have to pay rent man this week.
Father: I wasn't going to pay rent man. I was saving that money for a budgie.

A 'twenties' tune bursts out. The stage fills with dancing boys and girls, singing and dancing the 'Charleston'. There is a brief moment of life and light. This passes, and we are left with the family in the gloomy backstreets.

Father: Come on, grab your things. We're moving.
Mother: Where to?
Father: Albion Yard.
Mother: But them houses are condemned.
Father: Well, they're condemned here. As far as I'm concerned. Go on, get the handcart. Pile all the stuff on it.
Mother: You'll not get away with it. You'll need a paid up rent book.
Father: Oh aye. Here boy. *He calls the young boy to him.* Know what this is? It's a rent book. Pick it up, and drop it on the fire. *The boy does so.* That's right. An accident like.
Mother: They'll catch up with you one of these days.
Father: They know where to find me.

They pile all their stuff on to the handcart, and start laboriously to move away.
Pictures of industrial landscapes.
Screen : 1929.
Screams are heard. The stage area is filled with people in exaggerated poses of agony. People are, if possible, dropping from heights. The family continue their laborious trek.

Mother: What's all this?
Father: Search me. *He asks someone wailing.* What's up mate?
Man: Haven't you heard? It's the Wall Street Crash. Everybody's lost money.
Father *shakes his head:* It means nowt to me.

Another picture of a derelict area.

Father: Right here we are. Unpack our things.
Mother: What a place.
Father: It's the best I can do. There's no work.
Mother: 'Ere, what were that lot on about? What's the Wall Street Crash?
Father: Something to do with money I think. I think the world's gone broke.
Mother: Well we have. I know that for a fact. You'll have to go down the dole.

Fourth improvisation

Screen : Pictures of out of work men lounging up against walls. People walking through dismal streets. Music : Noel Coward sings Every little bird can fly *(on record MFP : The Master Sings).*
The acting area is filled with men and women walking around in circles. They have old clothes on. They stoop to pick up dog-ends, etc. They circle around until they have joined each other. They form a queue. The one at the head turns to the others, shakes his head and says, in an officious voice, I'm sorry. I'm afraid you don't qualify. *This continues until each person has turned to the others. They then break away.*
A group of children break into the group playing tag. The game takes over. Everybody is playing tag.
Screen : 1931. They freeze.
Screen : THE MACMILLAN REPORT ON BRITISH INDUSTRY.

Voice: The country is on the verge of bankruptcy.
Voice: I suggest we cut government employees' money, and cut the dole.

Searching for jobs in the 1930's.

There is outrage amongst the people.

Voice: You're not cutting the dole. *They freeze.*

Voice: What are you going to do about it Mr. Baldwin?

A character walks through the crowd in a bowler hat.

Man: I have decided to form a National Government.

The people cheer very half-heartedly. Hooray.

Man: I think I'll call for an election.

Candidates press through the crowds with soap boxes. Vote for me. *They all call out. They freeze.*

One of the crowd: Here is the result. The Conservatives have been elected.

The crowd all put on top hats, rosettes. The girls carry fans. They stand still. The family are seen in their house area.

Boy: Why can't we have any books?

Mother: Books? They'll be the ruin of you. You don't want to waste your time on those things. Or your money. If you ever have any. Look what your dad's found here.

Boy: What is it?

Mother: Why boy. It's a wireless.

Sounds of tuning in. Squeakings through the air. As the tinny squeakings increase, we hear a pure, tenor voice sing. As he sings, all the people in the acting area start to dance.

Song: If you were the only girl in the world
And I were the only boy
Nothing else would matter in the world today
We would go on loving in the same old way
A garden of Eden, just made for two
With nothing to mar our joy
There would be such wonderful things to do
I would say such wonderful things to you
If you were the only girl in the world
And I were the only boy.

39

Fifth improvisation

There is the sound of marching feet.
Screen : The Jarrow crusade. 1933.

A succession of pictures of working men marching.
Faces of working men.
A group of children gather at one side. They start
by looking at the pictures. As the pictures progress
they start to play a game.
The sound of marching gets louder. The picture of
the crusade is held.
Another group of children start to play in another
part of the acting area. They play a different game.
The two groups are unaware of each other. But the
two groups are converging. Suddenly both groups
become aware of each other and stop.
The picture is removed from the screen.

One kid: Go and play somewhere else.
Another kid *from the other group*: Oh yeah.
1st kid: Yeah. Get back up to the slums where
you belong.

The two groups start to wheel round each other in
slow motion. From time to time one of them runs
into the other group and attacks one of the others.
Sudden darts of movement in the slow motion.
The two gangs get closer together. The action gets
quicker. They close in. They are fighting, kicking,
swearing. The gangs are locked together. They
freeze.

Screen : 1936. WAR IN SPAIN.
A Spanish Civil War song is heard in the distance :

> If you want to write to me
> You know where you can always find me
> On the wide fronts of Gandesa
> In the midst of every battle.

A group of soldiers carrying guns enters and stands
above the frozen group of children. Another group of
people, this time civilians with guns enter. The two
groups converge, as the children had done. In slow
motion, the soldiers force the civilians to their knees
and finally to the ground. When the soldiers have
won, the group in the middle slowly move. The
children break up their group.
One group look down on the others.

One kid: Ha. Ha. Beat you. Get back to the
other side of town where you belong.

One group go out. The soldiers move away triumph-
antly. The odd mixture of Spanish civilians and
kids pick themselves up.

Sixth improvisation

Leader: Right, scatter. Hide over there. We'll
get that lot.

They all disappear.
The first group creep stealthily back. They look
round and call back to their friends. Suddenly the
second gang appear and shower the first group with
stones, pebbles and sticks. An allotment owner runs
in.

Allotment owner: If you kids don't get out of
here, I'll have the law on you.

Both groups are still. The allotment owner goes. One
boy, who is the leader, turns on them.

Leader: Right, all of you. Line up. You too.
He points to a little girl. Right. We're
going to get the Germans see. Now.
To get to the Germans in that allotment man's hut over there, you have
to cross the allotment. Now. You've
got to balance on the cabbages, because if you fall off you'll get blown up.
Right. At five-second intervals. Go.

One after another, they walk across the space, as if
balancing on cabbages. Occasionally a girl falters.
Her friend steadies her. As they are all balancing on
cabbages, the allotment owner comes back.

Allotment owner: I thought I told you kids.
Get off. I'm calling the police.

The leader goes up to him and hits him on the head
with a bottle.

Leader: Run, Alan. Run. *The man falls to the*
ground.

Screen : WAR. 1939.
Group of children look startled.
Sound of sirens.

Seventh improvisation

The children sit as if they were on a bus. They put on
gas masks. They attach labels to their jackets.
A girl starts to cry.

Boy: 'Ere silly knickers. 'Oo you going to?
Girl: I don't know, but I don't want to go
wherever it is.
Boy 2: Oh shut up sis.

He puts on his gas mask.

Evacuation 1939. Note gas mask cases and labels.

Boy: 'Ere look at Ging' in his gas mask. He looks like a pig.

Everybody laughs.

Boy 2: Oh. Shurrup.
Boy: I feel sick.
All: Err!

The group breaks up, and they each go to different areas.

Boy *looking at his label*: Mrs. Fleetwood.
Girl: Mrs. Fitzpatrick.
Another: Mrs. Smith.
Another: Mrs. Blockley.
Another: Mrs. Cutts.
Mother *standing apart and speaking*: Dear Alan. Yer dad and I have decided that since the war 'as been raging for four months and Nottingham hasn't been hit by a bomb once, we've decided it'll be all right for you to come 'ome, so we're coming up to collect you on Saturday morning. Love. Mam.

All the children break from their positions. The sound of droning bombers. People with helmets, ARP outfits. Some searchlights.

Eighth improvisation

Screen : The Roxy. 1941. Vera Lynn sings. *Clapping. The Manager returns.*

Manager: Good evening, ladies and gentlemen, and welcome to the old Roxy. I hope you enjoyed the film you have just seen, which was 'Lassie come Home', starring Lassie and Elizabeth Taylor. Next week we have a very special treat for you, Boris Karloff in 'Dracula'.

The Usherette walks through the crowd. She says Carrots. Penny a bag. Carrots.

There is a fiendish hissing. A loud cackling noise. In the swirling searchlights, and flickering cinema lights, a number of people stand about in disconsolate

41

moods. From the side the cackling gets louder, and Dracula himself enters, wearing a Hitler moustache and a swastika. He flings up his arm in a 'Heil'. As he does so, each of those standing about does the same. Dracula goes up to each one, and bites him in the neck. The victim expires and falls to the ground. The final one is already lying on the ground. As Dracula gets down to bite his neck, the victim rises, produces a Union Jack and sings Rule Britannia, Britannia rules the waves. *He stands and starts to wrestle with Dracula. As he does so, the others rise up and start to sing:*

> Run rabbit, run rabbit, run, run, run.
> Don't give the farmer his fun, fun, fun.
> He'll get by, without his rabbit pie,
> So run, rabbit, run rabbit, run, run, run.

Dracula melodramatically hisses away.
The lights come up, and the cinema audience applaud. Cinema organ music plays as the audience files out. A bell rings. Children file in. They are in a classroom.
Screen: 1942.

Ninth improvisation (based on *Mr. Raynor the Schoolmaster*)

Enter Teacher.

Teacher: Right. Face front. Get out your bibles. No, don't open them. Handley. Right Handley, stand up.
Handley: Yes sir.
Teacher: Now Handley. Who was Moses?
Handley: What Moses from the Bible sir?
Teacher: Yes, Handley. Moses from the Bible.
Handley: I don't know sir.
Teacher: We've been studying this part of the Bible for a month Handley. How come you don't know?
Handley: I forgot sir.
Teacher: Forgot! You didn't know in the first place. Right Robinson. No, don't sit down, Handley.
Robinson: Yes Mr. Raynor, sir.
Teacher: Who was Moses, Robinson?
Robinson: The brother of Aaron, sir. A priest, sir.
Teacher: Very good Robinson. Did you hear that Handley?
Handley: Yes sir.
Teacher: What house are you in Robinson?
Robinson: Buckingham, sir.

Teacher: Very good Robinson. Take two stars.

Robinson does so.

Teacher: Right, Handley. Who was Aaron?
Handley: The brother of Moses, sir.
Teacher: Very good Handley. Now then, who was Moses?
Handley: I don't know sir.
Boy: Then the Lord said unto Moses,
            All the Jews shall have long noses,
            Excepting Aaron.
            And he shall have a square 'un,
            And poor old Peter,
            He shall have a gas meter.

The teacher coughs. Handley sits. Teacher turns back. Two of the children start to fight.

Teacher: I saw that Bullivant. Come out here.
Bullivant: He hit me first sir.
Handley: No I never.
Teacher: And now I'm going to hit you. Come here. *He flexes a cane.*
Bullivant: You're not going to hit me with that.
Teacher: Hold your hand out.
Bullivant: No.

There is a set-to between the two.

Bullivant: I'll get our big kid on to you.
Teacher: Sit down.
            Right. Open your Bibles at Exodus, Chapter 6. *Reads* 'Then the Lord said unto Moses (*titters here*), now shalt thou see what I will do to Pharaoh.'

A bell rings.

Teacher: Right. Dismiss.

Other improvisations

The work continues with improvisations and dramatisations of:
   The Bike (from the collection *The Ragman's Daughter*). The end of the Second World War. Joining the RAF for National Service. Sent to Malaya. Contracting TB. Going to a sanatorium. Starting to write. The publication of *Saturday Night and Sunday Morning* in 1958, and success.

c. The Navigators

The following outline and script is a series of impressions based upon the theme of the coming of the railways to Britain in the nineteenth century. The theme is vast and embodies every aspect of life in Victorian and pre-Victorian times. The railway boom was the start of one of the most dynamic of social changes, followed by the development later of the motor car, which has been largely responsible for many changes in twentieth century ways of living.

The outline given is an evocation of ideas and suggestion of presentation rather than a succession of facts. Some facts and personalities are included, and ideas for the use of techniques of sound, light, slide, film, music, mime and improvisation are mentioned. Further study and collections of material could expand the ideas into a documentary play. (Terry Coleman's book *The Railway Navvies* would be useful.) The impressionistic series of ideas given here could be followed.

Preliminary activities

Imagine you live in a small suburban house which is threatened with demolition because a motorway is to be built through the land. What would your attitude be to the constructors? How would you feel if you were moved, perhaps to a place you didn't like?

Imagine you live in a peaceful village. It is proposed to build a new airport to cater for the people of a big city. Your peace, your property, perhaps your reasons for living there are shattered. How do you feel? How do you react?

Make an outline of the changes that occurred in people's lives in the nineteenth century (include such things as transport, industrialisation, public health, education, parliamentary reform).

Read stories and exploits of people of the time. Write out brief histories of Isambard Kingdom Brunel, George Stephenson, Thomas Brassey, George Hudson. Find examples of conflict (e.g. in the building of the lines through the West country).

Find out about the navvies themselves. (*The Railway Navvies* by Terry Coleman gives a detailed background and history.)

Find and collect anecdotes and quotations from the period, e.g. *Letter in the 'Birmingham Gazette' 1825*.

Do, good Mr. Editor, lend you potent aid at the commencement of the year, to avert the mass of evils, and help by advice, by entreaty, by warnings, by ridicule, by anything to thwart the designs of those iron-hearted speculators, who would take from the people of this country all hopes of another Merry Christmas.
signed 'Common Sense'.

Letter in 'The Times', 1843.

The railway smoke will spoil the fleece of my sheep.
Signed George Jones.

Twenty miles an hour! Why, you will not be able to keep an apprentice boy at work . . . Grave plodding citizens will be flying about like comets.

Investigate the use of masks, stylised movement (such as slow motion, large expansive movements, the movement of men involved in heavy labouring jobs), slides, film, light and music. (Refer to the section on 'Workshop'.)

Go out and meet labourers. Talk to them. If possible record their speech.

Keep a folder of nineteenth century happenings, especially those connected with the development of the railways. Expand sections in the following outline to include the information and material you have found. Try to re-envisage the straightforward facts in terms of drama methods, using some of the techniques suggested.

An acting space. Two suggestions of environment.

(a) Trestles, wooden beams, metal, rope, machines, pickaxes.

(b) Silk, chandeliers, ornate finery, delicate columns.

Two kinds of light.

(a) Warm, mellow, and bright.

(b) Cold, harsh, and dark.

The brightness and silk atmosphere in the centre of the acting area. The darkness and toughness at the outside. The noise of revolution, then of battle is briefly heard. Then dies.

Enter five people as into a room. High and curtained. A flickering light from a fire.
Distant explosions.
Enter a stately, frock-coated man. He goes to one of the people standing there and murmurs something in a low voice.
Distant crowds are heard.
The people look at each other. They are all unhappy. A girl quietly sobs. She buries her face in her hands. A man goes to comfort her.
The noise outside continues.

One man: He's dead. He was a good man.

Old lady: He was an old man.

Explosions continue and get louder. Flickering fires can be seen beyond the room. The sound of crowds swells.

Old lady: His Lordship is dead. Out there, celebrations for a different ending.

Man: Bonaparte defeated. Waterloo. A new beginning.

The crowd noises are reaching a peak.

Girl: Peace.

The noise swells. The family group stand. Darkness falls on them. Fires flicker. Explosions and fireworks. The family group are seen in the flickering fires. They are swallowed up in the rising sounds, the rising fires. The darkness at the sides breaks open into light. A violent cheer. Bursting noise, vitality, crowds. Fires, flags, people. Drums. Hooters. A wooden wrestling booth is placed in the centre. Two men wrestle. Great cheers.

Referee: Ladies and gentlemen. Tonight is Victory night.

Cheers.

Referee: Tonight we're celebrating here in London, and people are celebrating throughout the land. You've seen the bonfires burning. You know why. The French have been defeated.

Cheers.

Referee: In every corner of the land, bonfires are burning, drums are being beaten. Pipes played. God is on our side! The winds of the future are blowing our way.

Cheers

And tonight we have Tom Harrison of Stepney and Robert Newsome of Bow in the ring, and may the best man win there too.

Cheers.

The two wrestlers climb into the ring and the crowd cheers loudly. People surge about. Sounds of music, laughter, dancing. People eating, drinking, begging, stealing.
Soldiers walking with girl friends. Some limping, some on crutches, some blind. Gentlemen in top hats, ladies picking their way through the crowds.

Two gentlemen

1: Ha! Ha! Ha! What a great evening! A great victory! A great man Wellington! Finished him off. Could have made it last longer. I've lost money. Made more uniforms than they wanted. But, they'll need an army still.

2: I hope so. Hope they keep it up somewhere. Otherwise I'll lose a fortune on my guns. Still guns'll always be needed, keep the French in order or those damned rebel Americans.

The celebration swells.

2: Damned noise. Can't stand it. Look forward to going down to Dorset to the country.
Look at the fools celebrating. What have they got to celebrate? Half of them will be out of work now.

The wrestling match continues. Cheers. Jeers. A soldier and his girl in the crowd.

Girl: Ted. It's good to have you home.

Soldier: Yes.

Girl: Look at the fireworks.

Soldier: Like gunfire.

Girl: No silly. This is a happy evening. You're home at last, and the war's over.

44

Soldier: Of course, the suffering's over.

Girl: Ted. What's the matter?

Soldier: The war's over—it's the peace. What do they want with soldiers now? They don't want me, that's for sure.

Girl: Ted. It'll be all right. You'll see. You'll get a job. Don't worry.

The wrestling match finishes.

The referee goes to the centre of the ring, raises the hand of the winner. Loud cheers.

Referee: The winner (*hooray*).
Let's have three cheers, for
King George (*hiphip*)
Wellington (*hiphip*)
England (*hooray!*)

The cheering rises to a climax and breaks.

The crowds fall away. The central area is lit brightly. Parliament.

1st politician: We must rapidly get this country on its feet. Put it back where it was. The peace of rural England has been disturbed, but not shattered. We have a glorious future. The nineteenth century will be the most exciting in the history of mankind. Already we can see our supremacy over other nations demonstrated on the field of Waterloo, and soon we shall see our supremacy here in England. The development of the modern machine will lead us forward into a new age, and will help restore to us the things we love, back to stability and reassurrance.

2nd politician: I would like some reassurance about the 'modern machine' and the new age. I have recently travelled throughout the land in an effort to see signs of the new age. Gentlemen, all I see are peaceful villages, in which people work in their homes or on the large estates. The entertainment of the travelling fair alone disturbs the quiet. Not even the war with France has reached the quietest corners of our land. This 'new age' is a myth. It is true that in Wylam in the North, I saw demonstrated a form of engine operated with steam, but it was clumsy, expensive and noisy, and not very efficient.

As for other happenings, an unsuccessful attempt to build a tunnel under the River Thames, a slow but inevitable development in the manufacture of cottons and linens in special buildings away from the home, and the real advance in agricultural techniques constitutes nothing very remarkable in the way of the 'new age' or the 'machine age'.

3rd politician: It is true, is it not, that our soldiers, returning from the war, have easily found re-employment?

2nd: Absolutely. Back on the land. Or indeed in the new manufactories appearing in Lancashire. Some indeed were employed in the attempt to build the tunnel.

1st: Some also died in the attempt.

3rd: Who dreamed up such a crack-pot scheme?

2nd: A Mr. Brunel.

3rd: Brunel?

1st: A Frenchman.

3rd: French?

2nd: And his son.

1st: Isambard Kingdom Brunel.

A deep boom. Whispers are heard. Gloom descends. The voices whisper clearly. Isambard Kingdom Brunel. Is-am-bard King-dom Bru-nel.

Silence. Darkness.

Noise of water. Shapes are seen in the gloom. Hacking. Grunting. Water. A cry. Darkness.

A screen: Pictures of men working. A picture of Brunel.

The sound of crunching, drilling, smashing, darkness. A dim glow. The navvies are seen as shapes, hacking, crouching, coughing, spluttering. There is a moaning from them. A sudden spluttering sound. Light floods the area.

A tribunal has been set up. Dark-coated top-hatted gentlemen sit confronting panting navvies. The dark-coated men snarl viciously.

The screen shows Brunel again.

The two groups of men, navvies and tribunal confront each other. They snarl at each other. As they snarl the picture is changed.

Sound: A train shunting.

Snarl.

Screen: Men digging tunnel under the Thames.

Sound: Train shunting.

Snarl.

Screen: Lush open green fields.

Sound: Train moving slowly.

Snarl.

Screen: A manor house.

Sound: Train speeding up.

Snarl.

Screen: Another manor house.

Sound: Train whistling and going fast.

Snarls/trains and pictures flashing backwards.

I. K. Brunel, Engineer.

Stop.
Screen : An early train.
Sound : Train very rapid. Snarling very fierce. The men get closer together. Shots of Brunel, country-side, early train, manor houses, men digging flash by. The sounds of the train gets faster and louder. The men are locked together in controlled fury, grappling with each other.
A train whistle. All movement stops.
The picture of Brunel appears again and is held. One of the members of the tribunal stands, puts on his black stovepipe hat. Goes to a desk. One of the 'navvies' stands. They confront each other.

Tribune: You worked with Mr. Brunel and his father on the construction of the ill-fated Thames tunnel. You now have transferred your loyalty to Mr. Brunel's interest in the new contraption of Railway locomotives. You have, by doing so, brought a fresh menace to the land. Your behaviour is outrageous. What you do is destroy our peace and our land.

The other tribunal members have got up slowly and joined the one at the desk. All the Navvies, except the one standing, remain on the ground.

Tribune: Many of you fought in the war to save this land and to restore it to peace. Against the French. Mr. Brunel himself is the son of a Frenchman. That doesn't impress you. But you are bringing war to this country. The revolution that caused bloodshed in France has reached these shores. The galloping of horses heard in Manchester at Peterloo . . .

A series of pictures of people being slaughtered at Peterloo accompanies the remainder of this speech.

. . . now has become the sound of a railway engine, charging across the land. Our way of life is disrupted, we are put off our land. The railway means danger.
Your Mr. Brunel is a dangerous man. You navvies are dangerous men. You threatened us. Our holdings, and our families are at your mercy. We, who since time began, have been your leaders and your guides, are in danger from the machine. And if we falter, then your foundations will crack. You men will lose the security of our leadership, and you will not be able to judge the harm you will do yourselves.

As he finishes speaking, a picture of the Peterloo massacre is held. The tribunal stands 'frozen'. The navvy stands and looks at them, the others on the floor.

A group of poverty stricken women and children appear and stand near the navvy.

They sing :

> Pity the poor broken hearted,
> Unfortunate scamps that we be
> What we get shall be equally parted
> And spent in the first pub we see.

The tribunal is taken aback. The women shuffle off. The tribune clears his throat. Looks around for any more such groups to appear, convinced himself that they won't and continues.

Tribune: There are those among you who owe allegiance to Mr. Stephenson. I respect the man. He is an illiterate who, through application and diligence, has made good. He is an example to you. He deserves to succeed. The little engine he started at Wylam in the colliery there has been developed into an extraordinary machine.

We have room for those of you who can make good. We can help those of you in trouble. You must see that. For your poor women and children, for example, we can give shelter, in the workhouse nearby.

I beg of you men. Do what you did in France. Support our country. Otherwise you are guilty of bringing about civil war.

He sits. Formidable, with the other members of the tribunal looking down. A crack of thunder. The navvies herd together. Their leader looks at the tribunal.

Navvy leader: France is a long time ago. Nearly ten years. Forget the past. We're fighting battles now against the elements—getting roads of iron across Chat Moss swamp: digging tunnels and embankments. It's hard, dangerous work. The rain beats into the mud. The tunnels can crash down on our heads. You call us wild and lawless. We need to be. We're building roads out of the murky present into the future, which can't be worse. Locomotives will speed past old men, clinging to the past. You old men, sitting up there, will eventually make a lot of money out of us. You will gain from our hard work, and our deaths.

Tribune: You are trash. Foul-mouths, filthy scum. Your heathen like has never been seen on these islands before.

The navvy leader starts to chuckle, quietly. The others join in. The laughter spreads. There is general laughter. The members of the tribune begin to look alarmed. Some stand. They look hurt. Then they all sit. Bolt upright, like puppets on display. The navvies laugh loudly. The tribunal breaks up, members scattering. The navvies cheer. A band plays. Streamers. Music. Colour. A procession. The area is filled with people.

Screen : Picture of George Stephenson. It reads GEORGE STEPHENSON.
Screen : Picture of the Rocket. It reads ROCKET.

The band plays. A central platform is decorated with streamers. The area is crowded with jostling people. A barker stands.

Barker: Ladies and gentlemen. I crave your indulgence for a moment. A word of warning. Today is an historic day. The railway trials. The Rainhill Trials. I give you four competitors. Number one in the copper and blue colours, 'The Novelty', from Messrs Braithwaite and Erickson of London. Number two in the green, yellow and black: 'The Sans Pareil', from Mr. Ackworth of Darlington. Number three, yellow, black and white, 'The Rocket', Mr. Robert Stephenson. Fourth, 'The Cycloped', worked by a horse, Mr. Brandeth of Liverpool.

Cheers. Flag waving.

Bookie: Lay your bets here.

Barker: Now ladies and gentlemen! Keep away from the rails, keep to the sides. These locomotives are lethal. Sir. Sir. Please keep to the sides.

People gasp and clear right away, leaving the man in the middle and the navvies watching.

Barker: Now the trials are beginning. Perhaps you gentlemen would assist me in this. I've got three ropes here. Here you are. You lot are the 'Rocket' *he gives them a rope*; you lot the 'Novelty' *he gives them a rope*, and you lot the 'Sans Pareil' *he gives them a rope*. It looks as if the 'Cycloped' has galloped away. Right. Are you ready ?

The men stand with their three ropes, parallel. A group of three or four each stand and pull the rope taut. They start to pull. Others in their 'team' who are standing watching, start to make groaning

The Rainhill trials.

sounds, with great effort. The three trains start. The 'Rocket' isn't doing too well. The ropes slowly move forward. As they move forward, the train sounds from the three onlooking teams increases, depending upon the degree of success of the train. The 'Novelty' gets ahead. The crowd at the side cheers. Suddenly the men holding the rope falter and fall over. They slowly fall on to their sides. In slow motion. The second rope is coming up. The 'Rocket' is having a hard time. Some people shout, 'Come on Rocket'. Then it starts to gather speed. The 'Sans Pareil' develops some problem and starts to go very slowly. The team make appropriate sounds. The 'Rocket' picks up, and starts to overtake. For a few minutes the two are side by side. Great excitement. Then the 'Rocket' overtakes. The 'Rocket' gets to the winning post amidst cheers, bands, flags.

Barker: Ladies and gentlemen. The winner. Mr. Stephenson's 'The Rocket'. At (*he consults his watch*) 29 miles an hour, at its fastest. And an average of 14 miles an hour.

Great cheers. The navvies panting, stop. They all let out a huge cheer.

Navvy: Let's go for a beer lads.

Huge barrels are rolled in, and the men quickly drink large mugfuls of beer, whilst singing and dancing fill the area.

Navvies: Give us a song. Come on give us a song.

On to the little platform from which the Barker spoke, a small group of mimics assemble. They sing a noisy song. There are great cheers at the end.

Navvies: Hooray. Let's have more beer.

The navvies drink more beer. There is great noise and merrymaking. Two gentlemen enter and stand at the side.

1st: Look at them, disgusting creatures.
2nd: They are depraved, degraded and reckless.
1st: One can hardly call them Englishmen. They are a wandering people. Heathens in the heart of a Christian people. Savages in the midst of civilisation.
2nd: The boys are as bad. They ape the vices of the men. They swear, smoke, fight, and reel

48

through the streets at an age when, in other classes, they are under strict supervision.

A burst of noise comes from the navvies, who are inducing one of the women into a particularly wild dance.

Navigator: Right, now we've got the contract lads, we'll all be celebrating at the opening of the Liverpool–Manchester line.

Silence. Everybody is still.
Sombre drum beat.

A top-hatted gentleman: On the 15th of September 1830 will occur the most resplendent ceremony the world has yet seen. The launching of the Liverpool–Manchester railway. Such is the significance of the occasion that the Prime Minister himself, the Duke of Wellington (*boo from the Navvies*), the hero of Waterloo (*voice: And the villain of Peterloo*), will be there to open the proceedings. The Liverpool member of Parliament, Mr. Huskisson, has organised the whole affair, which will be jolly and gay.

Sombre drum beat.
The navvies assemble, very rigidly, in two lines.

Navvy 1: They'll all be there. The Lords and the Ladies, in their finery. *Drum.*

Navvy 2: We built the lines. *Drum.*

Navvy 3: We died in the tunnels and the embankments. *Drum.*

Navvy 4: The rails are painted in our blood. *Drum.*

Navvy 5: He'll be there. The Duke. In his faded glory. *Drum.*

Navvy 6: With the Lords and the Ladies. *Drum.*

Navvy 7: Will we get the vote? *Drum.*

Navvy 8: Who built the rail? *Drum.*

Navvy 9: Will we get to Parliament? *Drum.*

Gentleman: The Duke is ready. The trains are ready. The 'Rocket' is starting now.

We hear cheers and bands. We see two rows of dark-faced navvies.

Gentleman: There are crowds. Cheering. Everywhere, as far as I can see. Between them are the tracks. Three locomotives are ready to celebrate the opening.

A cannon sounds.

The 'Northumbrian' is moving along the track.

This is a fantastic, historic occasion. The noise is tumultuous. The train is moving out of sight. Here comes the Duke's special. It is slowing down. It has stopped. Some of the distinguished visitors are getting down to stretch their legs. Surely not. Can't they see? 'The Rocket' is approaching at great speed. Get in. Get in. Get back on the train. The visitors are scrambling to get back on the train. Two have got on to the train. Two have flattened themselves against the side as the train rushes forward. Look out Mr. Huskisson!! Mr. Huskisson has been caught by the passing train. It is stopping. The wheels went right over Huskisson's legs. The triumphant opening of the line has developed into tragedy. The poor man is being carried on to the train. Which is speeding back to the hospital. The Duke's train goes forward.

The navvies have stood stonily throughout this. As it ends they mumble.

Gentleman: The railway era has started.

The navvies are joined by a herd of people in shawls and poor clothes. They stand and confront the spectators. The mumbling grows to a roaring. They carry banners 'REMEMBER PETERLOO', 'PARLIAMENTARY REFORM NOW', 'VOTES FOR ALL'. *They start to throw brick bats, stones. A great surge of rhythm bursts forth.* Go back Wellington. Get out Wellington. Resign, Wellington. *As the noise rises, the group rushes forward, angrily shouting and throwing stones. As it reaches the front of the area, it stops, and the crowd freeze.*

Gentleman: The railway era has started.

A whole group of rough looking labourers assemble, with tools, pickaxes, packs, wearing rough woollen and moleskin-like trousers, felt hats. They make a tight and large group. They start to make a mumbling noise. They huddle together.
A message on a screen reads: The labourers came in troops from the fens of Lincolnshire, the wild hills of Yorkshire and of Lancashire. They poured in masses from every country of the Empire.
The mumbling rises to a formidable chanting. Jostling, nudging, getting in a group, they almost sing in rough voices.

Well we're off
We're off to build the railways

For the men
Who'll fight the landlords
Build the iron roads
Mr. Brunel
Mr. Stephenson father and son
and Mr. Brassey
We're off
For the wages that we'll get
From Mr. Hudson.

Navvy leader: Brunel's lot over here. Stephenson's here.

They stop chanting. Divide into two groups.

Leader of Brunel's group: Mr. Brunel is a great man. That we all know. It's undeniable. *The men agree.* He says that the narrow gauge is small, wastes time, space and money. He says that all over the world they'll be using the wide gauge. And he says we're going to build the railway from London to Bristol, right through some of the richest land in England. On the wide gauge.

Leader of Stephenson's group: Mr. Brunel is a clever man. But who built the 'Rocket'? Who won the Rainhill trials? Who is an Englishman? Who taught himself to read and write? Mr. Stephenson. And he knows engines. He's not just a clever speculator. He's a hard-headed engineer. The railway from Liverpool to Manchester is on narrow gauge, from Manchester to Birmingham is on narrow gauge, from Birmingham to London is on narrow gauge. Mr. Stephenson says that the whole country will be on narrow gauge.

Leader: Get the rope.

The two teams get locked in a tug of war. They are straining away.
A member of Parliament enters.

Member of Parliament: Stop. Stop all this. It's a bore. You railway navvies are the most ignorant men in the world. You go down tunnels none but the devil would enter, and you risk life for these maniacs. Don't you see you are ruining the peace, the beauty of the land.

The two teams stop, listen, then ignore him and carry on pulling.
A lady enters.

Lady: Stop. Oh do stop. I was visiting the vicar for tea the other day. We had just started on the cream, when the sound of a thousand devils filled our ears, and the room was filled with a vile black smoke. The devil, said the vicar, is loose. And he preached against it on Sunday. The devil is loose. Stop you men. You are giving in to the demon. You drink and swear. You are emissaries of the devil.

They pick up the rope. Enter a business man.

Business man: Go on lads. Pull. See who'll win. The genius from the south or the hard-headed one from the north. Go on pull. I'm banking on Stephenson. He always wins. I've bought up quite a few of the lines he's laid. I'm quite a rich man now. Started as a draper. Just goes to show. You need to see an opportunity and then take it. Pull lads.

The two teams pull. The Stephenson one is gaining ground. The teams circle round, and round. They sink to the floor. The contest is not yet won or lost. Lights fade. Silence.
A drum beat.
Enter rich landowner, wearing top hat and a mask. He stands legs apart. Enter navvy. He too wears a mask. Ferocious.

Landowner: Get off my land.
Navvy: I've come to build the railway.
Landowner: Go. *He points.*

Enter engineer, wearing a mask. He carries a bag with MONEY *written on it.*
Engineer jangles moneybag.
Landowner protests but takes money.
Engineer orders navvy to get to work. Navvy takes a pick and starts. Engineer stands with legs apart. One of the women, wearing 'sandwich boards' with a train painted on it, shunts by.
From behind the sandwich board she gives the engineer an even bigger bag of money. Rich landowner sits in the background, fuming, jangling his money bag. Engineer gives navvy money from his new bag. Navvy goes away happily, sits with a large bottle, drinks. Engineer puffs cigar.
After the first train has made its appearance, the scene is slowly repeated all over the stage, until there are locomotives puffing, navvies drinking, rich landowners fuming, and engineers jangling money bags.

Screen: A map. England. Black areas for Manchester, Liverpool, Birmingham. Map changes. Black areas get larger. Pictures of poverty, slums and railways. Mills, factories, smoke.

A contemporary print of a 'navvy' wearing moleskin trousers and a felt hat.

A thick smoke descends on the whole scene, which is getting very noisy (puffing, jangling, drinking). Everybody coughs. Much spluttering. The navvies start to lash out. They overturn trains, scatter money. People, objects, are wading through wreckage and clouds of smoke, coughing.

Above it all dangles a large carnival figure of Queen Victoria, glittering and forbidding. Her jewels are resplendent. It glints in the light. It is a scene of confusion, noise and contrasting colours. It subsides. People are lying around in the debris of smoke, trains, money and masks, Victoria swings on high. The navvies stand and walk through the debris.

Navvy leader: Rubble. That's what they're making of everything. Rubble. It would be possible to go forward, to progress. It is possible for people to have better lives. These were great men who worked and invented these things. But the bubble burst. Come on lads. Where's that rope? Who's going to win?

They pick up the rope, and through the debris, with Victoria hanging down, they start pulling the rope. The gentleman, the lady and the business man watch the contest. The Stephenson group win. There is much cheering. The Stephenson leader turns to the Brunel leader.

Stephenson leader: Never mind lads. There's plenty of work here. We've got to cover the whole country with railways. Brunel was a genius, but he didn't win. Your one wide gauge line to the West country will have to be changed. Come on over.

The sound of railway wheels on lines. The men slowly pick up axes, pickaxes. They rhythmically start to work. The great gangs are seen working hard away.

Screen: Pictures of changing housing conditions in England in the nineteenth century. Pictures of people changing. Pictures of developing railways.

Victoria is there still. The sound of railway wheels can still be heard.
Suddenly there is a loud booming sound. All freeze. Sounds of crunching metal. The people scream, and start to run about. They create a scene of confusion. Lights flash, as if fires are burning.

Voices: Disaster. Tunnels are collapsing. Trains have crashed. Help. People are being killed.

A band can be heard playing. The confusion dies.

The band plays a lively polka. People start to dance. There is much happiness. As the dance reaches a climax, there is another, louder crash. Again the lights flicker, again the sound of metal. Some people run around, the others stay still.

Voices: Explosions. Bridges are falling. People are dying.

Many take no notice. Another band starts to play, and the people continue to dance. The sound of more disasters is mixed in with the sound of continuous dance music. Some people look up and stop for a minute, but most carry on dancing. The area fills with a flickering light, as of fires. The music fades into a series of discordant crashes and booms. The people still continue running and dancing, cheering, shouting and laughing. The crashing and flickering get louder. They work their way to the edges of the acting area, the centre is clear. On the edges there are dancing figures in flickering firelights. Five people come and stand in the middle of the area, which is now brightly lit. It is the centre of a room, the movement around is dim but still visible.
The five people are mid-Victorians. Three are industrialists, one a painter and one a writer. The industrialists stand in a pose of dignity and authority, the flickering fire warms them. The painter sets up his easel and looks at the shapes in the gathering gloom. The writer picks up his pen, and speaks.

The writer: They do not hear the disaster any more. They only see the fireworks, the games. They know the machines mean money for them. They need the money. The poverty we see everywhere is slowly going. The rich are levelling out. It's all changing. But what is it changing into? *Boom.*
They can't hear the disaster. They are steering us towards something they can know nothing about. *Boom.*
We've got to tell them. We've got to go out and show them. Some of us have got to. Otherwise the machine will bring destruction. Not life. *Boom.*

An outburst of laughing, cheering, singing. Fireworks. Flames. The central group split and go off into different parts of the surrounding gloom. Two of them go towards Victoria, loosen the rope holding her and slowly lower her. They carry her into the gloom too. The whole area becomes filled with the fire. Flames leap up. We are left with the image of flames.

d. The Voyage of the Lucky Dragon*

The following is largely an adaptation of the book by Ralph E. Lapp and is an exploration of Japanese and American reactions at the time of the explosion of the hydrogen bomb on Bikini Atoll in March 1954. Many of the interpretative ideas suggested here were discovered in improvisation. The script here is also an indication; further dialogue can be invented while working on the ideas. The project may be improvised in units which are indicated by a line or cut-off across the script. The number of fishermen need not exceed more than six. Except for Kuboyama, the fishermen's names have been omitted to help recognition of function rather than character; the players should be allowed to develop their own.

The original improvised production included the use of 'Japanese' masks and 'American' masks as all players played both Japanese and American characters. The acting area was divided into approximately two even sides: one half of the area suggested Japan and the other half, America, with appropriate symbols drawn large in black on sheets of glued-together newspaper. The ship was indicated by a large decorated cardboard head of a dragon which later became the head of the festival dragon. The bomb was a dustbin placed on top of a tall pair of step ladders with torn paper inside which was scattered over the area, representing the dust, when the 'bomb' exploded.

Related reading

The Voyage of the Lucky Dragon Ralph E. Lapp, Frederick Muller

Kuboyama Richard Hudson with illustrations by Ben Shahn, Thomas Yoseloff

* Originally conceived in collaboration with Dan Garratt.

Films

The Japanese Fishermen commentary by Tom Driberg, distributed by Concord Films Council, Nacton, Ipswich, Suffolk

The Little Island a cartoon by Richard Williams

Prologue

Darkness

Sound: the high pitched hum of an approaching bomber. A date appears on a screen: AUGUST 5 1945. *The high pitched hum becomes a scream that cuts out at the climax.*

The date disappears leaving a white rectangle. Without sound we watch the bursting of an atomic bomb.

Darkness. Words flash onto the screen and quickly disappear.

FIRE STORM

ATOMIC DESERT

NIGHTMARE

Darkness

Words appear on the screen: RUMOUR. Approximately 100,000 civilians who were alive and unsuspecting at one moment were dead the next. The corpses uncounted—uncountable. The Americans record 80,000 people killed, the Japanese 200,000.

Voices: We the survivors of Hiroshima . . .

Voice 1: The trees and grass will never grow again.

Voice 2: The bomb emitted poisoned gas.

Voice 3: Within months of the explosion some of the babies were born with abnormally small heads.

Voice 4: Employment? Difficult . . .

Voice 5: Marriage? Impossible . . .

Voice 6: Any minor disease may be our last. Even if I sneeze people watch me.

Voices: We are untouchable . . .

The words fade as Bill Haley's version of 'Rock around the Clock' blasts out.

Screen: **The Harbour Town of Yaizu, Japan**

Thursday, January 21, 1954
Coloured lights, balloons, artificial blossom. People dancing, drinking, talking, a young couple begin to

dance exuberantly, clapped on by the others. Rock
around the Clock *comes to an end. Laughter. Applause. The next record is less dynamic. Some people
dance, others sit on tatami mats. No one is wearing
shoes; a row of assorted shoes line one side of the
acting area, some of the girls are clad in kimonos,
few carry fans. However this is Japan of the 1950's,
a mixture of ancient traditions and superstitions and
twentieth century technology. It is almost ten years
since the end of the second world war.*

Girl *to young man drinking*: Come on now.
       You've had enough. And you're sail-
       ing tomorrow morning.

Young Man: But I've only just come back and
       tomorrow is the first voyage of the
       New Year. *He grasps another jar of
       saki.*

Girl *snatching from him and throwing it to another
       girl*: You must be sober. You must
       catch lots and lots of tuna.

*Other girls join the game while the young man tries
to capture the jar.*

Young Man: Come on now, I missed the New
       Year celebrations and I shall be away
       for three months. Tonight is my night
       *and he launches himself amongst the girls
       and there is a tussle on the floor.*

*The giggling and the squirming calms down. Some
people leave. The young man is ringed by four girls.
The music is now that of a tinkling samisen and the
stately beat of wooden sticks. The action has become
formal. A girl offers the young man the jar of saki.
He drinks one long draught and passes the jar back.
Slowly and ceremoniously the girls remove the
young man's socks, his shirt, his trousers which they
fold neatly, and then lead him out of the acting area.*

Screen: **The Harbour Town of Yaizu**

*Friday, January 22, 1954. 10 a.m.
Sound: A cold wind.
A small crowd of well-wishers gather at the pier as
the crew make last minute preparations for their
long voyage. Some hold in mittened hands brightly
coloured balloons. One pushes on a pram, and carries
a Japanese sleeping mattress for her husband. The
radio man, Kuboyama, carries his radio, hurries
onto the ship, places the radio and returns to his
wife and collects a bundle of books. The cook runs on
grinning, he talks to the audience.*

Cook: I cook the meals on an ancient oil
       stove in a passageway. I don't even
       have a galley to myself. And him, the
       captain, puts his entries in the log at
       Tokyo Standard Time. I have to cook
       the meals according to stomach time.
       I don't know why I do it, but if the
       catch is good—everyone's happy.

*A large well-dressed man enters. He calls the Fishing
Master to him.*

Man: Fishing Master, I think it a good idea
       if you fished around the Midway
       islands.

Fishing Master: But that's over two thousand
       miles away, and the crew expect to be
       going to the Solomon Islands, the
       Midway can be dangerous.

Man: Look at these reports. *He takes papers
       from his pocket.* They're good, very
       good indeed. The Midway looks very
       rich.

Fishing Master *looking at the papers*: All right,
       but we must tell the Captain and the
       Radio Man.

Man: No, I don't think you need to do that,
       tell 'em on your way out. Besides they
       have nothing to fear, the ship is called
       'The Lucky Dragon', the symbol of
       good fortune and didn't I call it No. 5.
       Remember, to have called it number
       four would have been asking for
       trouble. Four sounds like our Japan-
       ese word for death. You really have
       nothing to worry about. The Midway
       will prove fruitful and you're Fishing
       Master of a lucky ship. Good luck.
       Make it a good catch. Remember I
       and the crew are relying upon you.
       He turns to the crew. Good luck men,
       have a good catch.

*Kuboyama the radio man, makes a last minute check
of his radio, the long aerial extended, and representing the mast of the ship. The Engineer attaches
coloured ribbons to the aerial, the other ends are held
by people standing on the pier, including the girls
from the restaurant. A loudspeaker blares out a
military march. The Engineer checks with the
Captain and signals for the engines to start. The
remaining mooring lines are cast off. The crew shout
and wave to their friends on the pier. 'Take care.'*

Japanese fishing boats in a typical small harbour.

'Take care of the children.' 'Look after your-selves.' 'Good catch.' *The engine sparks alive. The crewmen wave their cotton headbands. The girls from the restaurant wave excitedly. The older women wave but stand with more decorum. The two groups begin to widen the space between them. The loudspeaker plays 'Auld Lang Syne'. The paper streamers stretch and break and the 'ship' settles, gently rocking on the water while the group on the 'pier' slowly leave the area.*

Screen : **The Lucky Dragon clears Yaizu lighthouse**

Friday, January 22, 1954.

The Engineer approaches the Captain and explains that he has left a spare part on shore without which the engine will be useless if it were to break down.

Captain: But to return to port is not good. We have only just left. To go back now would be bad. None of us would take kindly to the jeers we would get if we went back. *He looks at a map.* If you really must have this spare part we'll put into Ogawa.
Hard-a-port.

The crew move round to show that the ship has changed direction. Suddenly the 'ship' jerks, and the engine cuts out.

Cook: We've run aground!

Captain *glares at the Engineer* : Get ashore and get that spare part—quick!

The Engineer leaps, as though over the side of the ship and runs. He soon returns carrying a piece of machinery.

Captain: We now have to wait for high tide to lift us off.

The crew wait crouched down—slowly they rise as though the sea is lifting the ship.

Screen : **The Pacific Ocean**

Sunday, January 24.
Sound : The chug of the boat, wind, the swash of the sea. The radio playing 50's 'pop' music.
The Fishing Master asks Kuboyama, the radio man, to turn the music off as he wishes to speak to the crew. The Fishing Master tells the crew of their destination. The men are surprised.

Cook: I thought we were off to the Solomon Islands.

Kuboyama: This is most unusual Fishing Master. It is customary to consult myself, the radioman, the Captain and the Chief Engineer before taking such a decision.

Captain: To the Midways in this old ship? It's expecting too much to go to the open sea to the east isn't it? But you're the Fishing Master, and even I, the Captain, must obey the decisions made by you.

Engineer: And the engine. It's not good enough. It might break down, and in rough weather this could be dangerous.

Fishing Master: We must risk that. Anyway I have faith in your skill as our engineer.

Engineer: But, Fishing Master, I cannot work miracles. We should go where we all agreed to go.

Murmurs of assent, agreeing with the Chief Engineer.

Fishing Master: The business of a fishing boat is to catch fish; therefore this boat must go where the fish are likely to be.

Captain: A hold full of tuna is what we all want —we don't want to return with nothing. We are all agreed on that. *The crew murmur agreement.* Return to work. And set course for the Midways.

The crew move to their stations : the radio is switched on. All face the same way and turn, suggesting the change of course. The wind rises and the ship moves into rough sea. The crew prepare the fishing lines.

Screen : **The Pacific Ocean**

11 p.m. February 5.

Fishing Master *standing up:* Stand by to throw lines.

The crew· prepare to throw. A ship's bell sounds. Pause.

Fishing Master: Begin throwing lines.

The lines are thrown. Action freezes.

Screen : **The Pacific Ocean**

7 a.m. February 6.

Fishing Master: Haul in the lines.

The men start by eagerly pulling the lines, then turn to the Fishing Master for the next instructions.

Cook: Where are the tuna?

Winchman: One sword fish will make little money.

Kuboyama: It's a poor catch. *They complete pulling in the lines.*

Fishing Master: Proceed East south East. *The engine chugs into life.*

Screen : **The Pacific Ocean**

February 9.

Sound : Engine chugging, a rising wind.
Flashes of light—lightning.
The figures of the fishermen curl and roll and jerk in sympathy with the storm. The noise of thunder and a howling wind.
The engine falters and stops. The crew look at each other in dismay. The storm dies. The sound of hammering upon metal and the engine splutters and chugs into life and fades. Silence.

Screen : **The Pacific Ocean**

February 12.

Sound : Wind, sea and the creak of a winch. The crew are seen hauling in the lines, their rhythm breaks.

Winchman: The main line's broken.

Fishing Master: We must search for the lost lines.

Cook: This is no place to fish. Why did we come here in the first place?

The engine chugs into life and the crew set to watch the sea for signs of their lost lines.
The Fishing Master dictates while Kuboyama taps out a radio message : AT . 1300 . LINES . CUT . SEARCHING ·. FOR . REMAINING . 240 . SETS . CLOUDY . 60 . SETS . FOUND . 180 . SETS . REMAIN . SUNK.

56

Fishing Master: Cease searching.

The crew relax and the Cook passes round drinks.

Winchman: Son of a deer and a horse. Why did he order us to come here against our will?

Kuboyama: What's the matter who's to blame? We will work for two months and have nothing to show for it.

Fishing Master: We still have enough line and fuel to make a good catch. I think we should go north where the high priced fish are.

Kuboyama: This old ship could not stand the rough seas of the north.

The Engineer: The main bearing of the engine has already burned out once.

Kuboyama: I think we should go south, to the Marshall Islands. Where the sea is calmer.

Fishing Master: But to go to the Marshalls will stretch our fuel supply.

Engineer: But the sea is calmer, the engine will not be under such strain.

Cook: We do not want to go home with an empty hold. The big eyed tuna swim near the Marshall Islands.

Fishing Master: All right, we'll go south.

Kuboyama: But if we do go south, we must keep clear of Bikini. That's where the Americans have their Atom Bomb tests.

Engineer: But the Americans haven't tested a bomb there since 1946. I think we should go south.

Fishing Master: Start the engine. Set the course south.

The engine splutters into life. The crew change physical direction to suggest change of course.

Screen: **The Pacific Ocean**
February 16. Weather clear. Catch fair.

Screen: **The Pacific Ocean**

February 20–26. Lines thrown eight times. Little caught.

Screen: **The Pacific Ocean. Near the Marshall Islands**

February 28.

Fishing Master: Throw lines.

The crew go through the actions of line throwing.

Kuboyama: Perhaps the new month will bring us luck.
Engineer: Then we will head for home.
Fishing Master: Are all the lines set?
Crew: Aye.
Fishing Master: Cut engines. Drop anchor.

The chugging engine stops, the crew relax. Kuboyama puts a record on the gramophone.

Screen: **Position of 'Lucky Dragon'**

Longitude: 166° 30′ E.
Latitude: 11° 52′ N.
100 miles East of Marshall Islands
14 miles outside boundary of restricted zone of US Government's Atomic testing area, Bikini.

Screen: **Sea: calm**

Weather: clear
Wind: E.N.E.
Sunrise: 6.09 A.M.

Screen: **6.12 A.M.**

Without sound we watch the explosion of an H-Bomb. Brilliant lights flash and oscillate and fade leaving a yellow-orange glow.

The crew leap to their feet and are silhouetted against the light.

Crew: The sun rises in the West.
Cook: That's impossible!
Engineer: It's a pikadon.*
Kuboyama: If it's a pikadon there should be a mushroom in the sky.

The sky darkens leaving a bright red disc of light.

Captain: What's the big red ball?
Engineer: It's a pikadon.

Pause, as the red disc fades. The sound of distant rumbling echoing and growing louder until it feels as though the whole world is shaking. The crew throw themselves on the floor. The sound fades.

Crew: What was it?
Cook: Don't know.

* *Pika-don* = Japanese for thunder-flash; a word born at Hiroshima when the A-bomb exploded there in 1945.

Crew: Could it be cannon fire?

Engineer: It's a pikadon . . . look how the clouds have darkened the sky.

Kuboyama: It was about seven minutes between the flash and the explosion, and if the speed of sound travels at a thousand feet a second, and estimating seven minutes we must be about 87 miles away.

The Fishing Master brings out his map; the crew gather round hushed, nervous.

Fishing Master: Look, we're about 85 miles from the centre of Bikini. That flash must have come from Bikini.

The Fishing Master looks up at the sky and turns to Kuboyama.

Fishing Master: Keep a sharp look out for any aircraft. The Americans may blast us out of the ocean.

Cook: Let's cut the lines and get out of here.

Fishing Master: No, wait. We lost lengths of line at the Midway. Surely we don't want to return to Yaizu with a poor catch and no line.

Cook: But what about that Japanese fishing boat that disappeared in 1952? It's still unexplained and if we stay here we too might be blown out of the sea by the Americans.

Fishing Master: We've not seen any aircraft, there's no sound of one and our line stretches away, away from Bikini and if we work fast we can haul in our catch and be away. I don't want to hang around here any more than you do.

The Fishing Master rings the bell.

Fishing Master: Start up the engines and begin hauling in the lines.

They set to work.

Captain: I don't like the look of the weather. Those clouds are black.

It begins to 'snow'. The crew pull their hats down over their eyes.

Kuboyama: It looks like the beginning of a snow storm.

The men continue to work hauling in the lines and go through the business of gutting and cleaning the fish.

Fishing Master *orders with bell and instructions:* Go ahead . . . Slow . . . Stop . . . Go ahead . . . Slow . . . Stop . . .

As the men work and it continues to snow. Some of the men complain that their eyes hurt and put on dark glasses.
Kuboyama looks carefully at the 'snow'.

Kuboyama: It looks like salt.

Others taste it.

Captain: It's some kind of white sand, falling from the heavens.

Kuboyama: You can't taste it or smell it.

Cook: Whoever heard of a sandstorm at sea?

The cook appears with a meal and one by one the men turn away from the food:

I'm not hungry.
I feel sick.
I have no appetite.
I've got a headache.

Cook: All lines aboard, Fishing Master.

Fishing Master: Start engines. Wheelman set course due North.

Kuboyama taps out message and as he taps the screen states: 6 P.M. LUCKY DRAGON RETURNING HOME.
Sound: The swash of water, chugging engine, a cold wind. Water and engine fade. Only the cold wind is heard as the light fades on the huddled crew.

Screen: **March 2, 1954. Washington, D.C. U.S.A.**

Sound: A military band plays loudly 'The Stars and Stripes' as the American flag is unfurled. A well-dressed American business man with horn-rimmed spectacles stands in front of the flag.

American: As Chairman of the United States Atomic Energy Commission I wish to announce that today, March the Second the Joint Task Force Seven has detonated an Atomic device at the Atomic Energy Commission's Proving Ground in the Marshall Islands. This detonation was the first in a series of tests.

The crew of the 'Lucky Dragon' come forward and sit cross-legged below the Chairman of the AEC, with their backs to him.

58

Crewman: I stayed in my bunk that day, too ill to help to clean the fishing gear and dry the ropes.

Winchman: When I woke that morning I was unable to open my eyes they were glued together by yellow discharge. Also the rubber bands that I wore around my wrist over my gloves when fishing, crumbled and fell in pieces.

Cook: We all complained of itchyness, particularly around the hands and neck. And when we handled the ropes, they felt as though they were burning.

Captain: No matter how much we washed and scrubbed the deck that white ash remained in corners, on the rims of portholes, between the buoys and it seemed to stick to the nets.

Engineer: I found sores around my neck and on my fingers, and I noticed we all looked unusually sunburned.

Kuboyama: I believe we must have encountered an atomic explosion.

Crewman: Kuboyama?

Kuboyama: Yes?

Crewman: Look I have collected a sample of the dust. It looks like white coral from an atoll. We could have the ash examined by someone when we get home.

Kuboyama accepts the packet and the crewmen return to form the shape of their ship.
Headline (a long sheet of paper unrolls with the words):

ATOM RAYS STRIKE 264 IN PACIFIC

A secretary runs onto the acting area and hands to the Chairman of the AEC who reads:

Chairman: We had also informed the Japanese Maritime Safety Board prior to these 1954 test series defining a forbidden area, which we believe to be quite sufficient.

Kuboyama: I maintained daily radio contact with Japan and I received no message about this announcement.

Japanese Official: I represent the Japanese Maritime Safety Board. It is true that we had been informed that the Americans were nuclear testing on the Marshall Islands in the Spring of 1954. However, there was no prior announcement of the actual date. The boat owner could have warned his ship had he known when and, indeed, if his ship was near the danger area.

He goes out.
Sound: 'The Stars and Stripes' as the flag of the USA is removed and the Chairman of the AEC exits.
Sound: A cold wind, water, chugging engine.

Screen: **The Port of Yaizu**

Sunday March 14. 5.30 a.m.
The Boatowner and a clerk from the Fishery Union stand on the pier as the 'Lucky Dragon' throws out its mooring ropes.

Fishing Master: We saw an atom-bomb test. Did you know there would be tests on Bikini?

The Captain: We have only made a very poor catch and we have lost many lines.

Boatowner: I'm more concerned for you than for the boat, or for the catch, or the lines. You had all better go to the hospital, immediately.

The fishermen cover their faces with towels and scarves and hurry through the back streets to Yaizu Hospital. It is a fair and warm Sunday. People are out walking and gossiping. Children playing. The fishermen did not wish to meet anyone. They had returned home without profit, suffering from a strange sickness.

Kuboyama: I am in better shape than many of the crew. With some of them their hair falls out. I am like this (*gestures to towel covered face*) because I am afraid to have people look at me. Wife! Wife!

Mrs. Kuboyama appears.

Mrs. K.: Welcome home. You must be very tired. Let's have a look at you. *Pause.*

Kuboyama unwraps the towel. Pause.

Mrs. K.: I can hardly make you out. You're the same colour as the wall. You're the colour of a Negro.

Kuboyama: I don't know exactly what happened, but on our way home we encountered an atom-bomb I think—no don't worry—we only saw its blast

59

and we were far away and we only ran into some ash. I will be well soon. Don't worry, I'm going to the doctor right now.

Screen : **Yaizu Hospital**

Kuboyama joins the group at the hospital. The crew stand ill-at-ease. A receptionist enters.

Receptionist: Yes, what do you want?
Fishing Master: We would like to see a doctor.
Receptionist: Don't you know today is Sunday?
Fishing Master: Yes, but we thought—
Receptionist: We refuse everyone here on a Sunday, except emergency cases.
Fishing Master: But we think we are an emergency. We all feel sick; we've just returned from fishing. We think we saw an atom bomb. We need to see a doctor now.
Receptionist: All right. I'll see if I can get hold of a doctor, but I can't promise he'll come.

The Receptionist explains to a doctor, who sits with his back to the fishermen.

Doctor: Tell them that it's Sunday, and if they want medical check-ups there's nothing I can do about it without assistance. Why don't they come back tomorrow and get treated by the duty doctor. You know that I'm a surgeon and physical check-ups are not my responsibility.
Fishing Master: No, tomorrow might be too late for all we know. We have crewmen who must be examined. We have just returned to Yaizu this morning.
Doctor *looking closely at the Fishermen:* What's all this about? What's the matter with you all?

He begins to examine them.

Cook: We think we saw an atom bomb explode. We heard a huge sound and later something that seemed like ash fell on our boat and we felt sick.
Doctor: Since you all came back safely I think you need not worry very much.
Fishing Master: The great flash of light was like dawn, but too early for dawn.
Doctor: Many were blinded at Hiroshima by

the flash. And this light that you saw, wasn't blinding?
Fishing Master: No.
Doctor: Then you must have been a safe distance away. Come again tomorrow and we'll have an examination with all the doctors here.
Boatowner: What about the fish that was caught? What shall we do with them? They've been carefully wrapped in vynl sheets and stored in the hold of the ship.
Doctor: The fish is yours and I don't think it will be necessary to check them. I have no geiger counter in the hospital, and I'm not unduly alarmed by your condition.
Fishing Master: Of course, we do not doubt your diagnosis doctor, and I'm sure we are all relieved to learn that we are not in serious trouble, however I think I should like to know the reasons why we are burned and why we are so out of condition. May we send some of our crew to Tokyo where we hear they have experts on atomic sickness. Would you be kind enough to write a letter of introduction?
Doctor *a little put-out:* All right.

The Receptionist brings writing paper and the Doctor writes.

Screen : **March 15. Tokyo**

A crowd of people, all bustle and no one idle; mothers busy with babies, old women jog-trotting, pedestrians scuttle, stall holders flick wares with feathered fans, sandwichmen advertise films, some people wear bandages over their mouths to prevent giving colds to others, a salesgirl eulogising into a microphone the benefits of makeup, a deformed beggar playing a flute, the street is alive with radio loudspeakers, motor car horns, some buying and selling in deaf and dumb show. A policeman stops and starts the crowds movement with the precision of the jerky animation of a bioscope film. Into this hectic picture wander the fishermen who ask their way to the University Hospital and are directed to a semi-circle of outpatients sitting on chairs. Section by section the crowd freeze. Silence. The fishermen are examined by a Professor.

A street scene in Tokyo.

The Professor: The whole clinical picture of the fishermen was acute inflammation which is usually caused by an overdose of soft X-rays.

Two men stand under a company title: Fuji Fisheries Company. *They drink mugs of tea. Behind them stands an eavesdropper.*

1st Man: Did you hear about what's happened at Yaizu? One of their ships got caught in a huge flash, and there was a strange thunder in the sky; apparently the men were burnt; and there was some curious ash-fall. And some of the crew have lost their hair . . .

As they turn away and the title disappears. Another group come to life under the title 'Yomiuri Shimbun—Newspaper'.
Sound: Typewriters.
A newspaper office. Editor at his desk answering phone; a journalist is correcting proofs, a girl waiting to take notes. The eavesdropper comes in and hurriedly talks to the editor who looks up and barks at the journalist.

Editor: A boat's been near Bikini . . . the crew's been covered with ash . . . the men were burned . . . some crewmen have come to Tokyo today . . . it's a big story . . . go to Tokyo University Hospital at once . . .

The space is cleared for the hospital.

Screen: **Tokyo University Hospital. March 15. Night**

The acting area now suggests a hospital, patients lying in rows under white sheets, nurses on duty; a defined area for the reception desk.

Journalist: Did the patients with the atomic disease come here today?
Receptionist: Yes, they were here today.
Journalist: Good. Can I see them?
Night Nurse: . . . No, on no account must they be disturbed.
Journalist: If it's impossible to see them, may I at least know their names?
Nurse: I see no harm in that. *She nods to the Receptionist who shows the Journalist the list of patients.*
Journalist *checking the list*: Thank you very much.

Nurse: I suggest you come back tomorrow.

The Journalist keeping very low and watching the Night Nurse, and others on duty, crawls amongst the sleeping forms whispering: Men from Yaizu. *Many patients are asleep, others shake their heads as the Journalist tiptoes round the hospital. Suddenly a body sits up.*

Journalist: Men from Yaizu?
Winchman: Yes.
Journalist: I'm from a newspaper. I'd like to know what happened.

Freeze.

Screen: **Tuesday, March 16**

Sound: A giant newspaper press is switched on, gathers momentum and thunders.

Journalist *shouts, waving newspaper*: Read this!

Screen: **Japanese fishermen encounter atomic bomb test at Bikini**

23 Men Suffering from Atomic Disease.
One Diagnosed Serious by Tokyo University Hospital.
H-BOMB?

Voices of Newsvendors: Fall Out Victims . . . Fall Out Victims.

Darkness.

A camera bulb flashes, revealing Kuboyama's radio with the aerial extended and a few strands of coloured streamers dripping from the top. Another flash, this time from a different angle. Someone with a torch attaches a newspaper to the aerial. People begin to gather. Some 'comfort girls' can be seen slipping away from some of the crewmen of the 'Lucky Dragon'. More reporters arrive and interview the crewmen, taking photographs from various angles, taking groups, individuals, cameras flash. A television camera appears with its attendant, interviewer, producer, continuity girl. The sound of impatient motor horns, as more reporters arrive. Carpenters arrive to do some repairs to the boat and begin to work. A doctor and an assistant appear, carrying a geiger counter. They work their way around the ship unnoticed by the busy reporters. Quietly the doctor begins to organise the fishermen into a group, everyone becomes aware that something unusual and important is happening as the doctor examines the fishermen with the geiger counter. All sounds die. The only sound that can be heard is the ominous clicking of the geiger counter.

Doctor: I never before encountered radio-activity like this; I have never dealt with anything of such potency before. This boat is extremely radio-active and this boat must be taken from this berth and placed in quarantine. Also I advise the crew to leave this boat pending further investigations and to become voluntary patients at the hospital.

The reporters and the newsmen begin to edge away from the fishermen, being careful not to touch them and then running to get the news to their newspapers and TV studios.
A notice is placed on ship : DANGER. KEEP AWAY.

Two 'comfort girls' run on calling : Doctor . . . Doctor.
A Doctor appears.

Two 'Comfort Girls': Oh, Doctor, we would like to have a consultation in a hurry. Last night we played with the crewmen of the 'Lucky Dragon' and we wonder if we are contaminated. If we're radio-active?

The Doctor examines them with a geiger counter.

Doctor: You are both all right; you're quite safe.
The two girls, thankful, hurry away.

Screen : **March 16. Osaka Fish Market**

Sound : Train pulling in and pulling out.
The space is organised into avenues and stalls and peopled by fish porters. They carry on their heads, wheel on trolleys, lift and place down, barrels, baskets, boxes of fish from incoming transport to the stalls. Vendors sell and auction fish, weighing, wrapping for customers, restauranteurs, sushi shops, landladies, mothers inspecting, bartering, buying, others packing, labelling, shipping. There is much noise.

Loudspeaker: Your attention . . . your attention please. This is important. Would all vendors who have a consignment of fish from Yaizu, please step forward and remain by their consignment. No one else is to move.

The vendors who have a consignment of fish from Yaizu move and stand by their fish from Yaizu. Officials in white coats appear carrying geiger counters.

Chief Official: We are from the Osaka City Health Office and we have been given to understand that the fish from Yaizu may be contaminated by radio-activity. All right, doctor.

A doctor comes forward with his geiger counter ; the instrument begins to tick and soon gathers into a furious high pitched rattle.

Doctor: It's running at 2,000 counts per minute!
Fish vendors, customers back away saying : The fish are crying.
The vendors whose fish had been examined ask : But what about our fish? What are we to do?
Another official appears : I have authority from the Ministry of Welfare who advise burying the contaminated fish.

Vendors/Customers: But this will ruin us, burying the fish.
Welfare Official: Over four thousand pounds of suspect fish were buried at dawn in Tokyo this morning. The suspect fish here should also be buried.
Vendor: But I've already sold some of the Yaizu fish.
Another Vendor: So have I.
Welfare Official: Then we must try to find the people you sold them to.

Officials from the Health Office organise the digging of a pit outside the market area and the search for the people who may have bought Yaizu fish. Workmen dig the pit and the fish are tipped into it as a vendor talks to the audience.

Vendor: This is just the catch from the 'Lucky Dragon'. What of all the rest of the fish in the sea? A tuna can travel 35 miles an hour. They will be standing here with their geiger counters for ever. And my business? What of that?

A sushi stand with vendor and customer, eating out of a paper wrapper.

Customer: If there is one thing we enjoy in Japan it's sushi. It's made of rice balls,

63

flavoured with hot green horse-radish sauce and decked with strips of raw, red tuna fish. We eat it rather like the English eat fish and chips. I'm told that we Japanese consume a million pounds of tuna a day and that there are as many as two and a half thousand sushi shops in Tokyo alone.

A fish shop and customer buying fish.

Customer: In America many families only have fish about once a week, but in Japan we rely upon fish as our main source of protein and eat fish practically every day in one form or another.

Manager of an Indian restaurant: Business is not so good. The Japanese seem to prefer their own food and cooking. It's not easy to get them to try Bombay duck, curried beef, keskebah. In fact unless a miracle happens I will have to close my restaurant.

Loudspeaker: Warning . . . warning . . . radio active fish from Yaizu. Radio-activity may have transmitted its poison to other shipments. Listen. This is the sound of the telegraphic clicks of a geiger counter reacting to radio-active fish recorded in Osaka market this morning . . .

The ominous sound of the geiger's rattle is heard, amplified. Newspapers and leaflets are quickly distributed. The customers quickly stop patronising the sushi and fish shops giving the fish back, throwing it away into dustbins and queuing up at the Indian restaurant. The sound of a sitar. The happy turbanned manager smiles and bows.

Manager: Business is now good. I have customers today who have probably never eaten a foreign meal in their lives. I must make them welcome so as they will come again.

Sitar music fades.
The sushi and the fish vendor have put up placards:
WE DO NOT SELL RADIO-ACTIVE FISH
EAT HERE. OUR FISH COMES FROM THE NORTH COAST

Sushi vendor: My trade is at a standstill.
Fish vendor: What can I do? Within one day my business has dropped. No one will have my fish—even if I try to give it

away. What will happen? We should get compensation.
Screen: RUMOUR. FISH IS FORBIDDEN FROM THE EMPEROR'S DIET.
They try without success to attract passers-by to buy their sushi and fish, as the Indian restaurant overflows with customers.

Placard: **H-bomb counter-measures headquarters**

A number of booths, each with a doctor and a geiger counter. Officials organise the crowd of people into queues. The conversation in the booths is similar and can happen simultaneously.

Booth one: I have eaten fish today and I'm afraid that I might be radio-active.
Booth two: I served some customers with fish from Yaizu. Will you please check me and then I will try to find the customers?
Booth three: I must have a thorough examination. I'm sure I've eaten some contaminated fish.
Booth four: I was eating some sushi with raw tuna which must have come from Yaizu. I'm sure I'm radio-active.

Each time the patient goes through the doctor says: You're safe. *The patient then goes to the Indian restaurant.*
When the customers have finished their meal they come out of the restaurant and walk home; the fish vendor and the sushi vendor try to sell their fish, again without success; they too pack up their stalls and go home.

Screen: **The home of the wheel-man of the 'Lucky Dragon'**

Sound: Samisen and wooden sticks.
A Japanese bathtub is brought on with the Wheel-man inside it soaping himself. As he is bathing, a neighbour calls to ask if he can have a bath. As this is the custom in certain areas of Japan the wheel-man agrees. His wife brings tea and takes a towel to her husband who comes out of the bath. The neighbour removes his gown and he too slips into the bath. Fuel is expensive, so the same water is used over and over again. As the neighbour is bathing so another neighbour arrives and also asks if he may have a bath; the second neighbour slips into the bath as the first neighbour climbs out. All is happy and congenial.

A family atmosphere, where friends relax with friends. As the second neighbour gets out of the bath two doctors arrive in white coats and with a geiger counter. The sound of the samisen and the wooden sticks stop.

Doctor One: Are you the wheelman of the 'Lucky Dragon'?

Wheelman: Yes. Can I help you?

Doctor One: We are here to collect the clothes you wore while at sea. They may very well be radio-active.

Wheelman: By all means. You will find them lying over the chair.

Doctor Two switches on the geiger counter and as he approaches the chair the geiger counter rattles. He also directs the counter at the bath; again it rattles much to the alarm of the two neighbours and their wives who insist on an examination, explaining that they had just had a bath in the wheelman's tub. The doctors oblige and declare the neighbours safe. However, there is obviously a change in the relationship between the neighbours and the wheelman. The neighbours hurriedly make excuses and go.

Doctor One: Also we would like you to come to the hospital now, with the rest of the crew.

They go.

Screen : **Yaizu Hospital**

The fishermen assemble and stand awkwardly waiting on the doctors; Doctor One explains that each one of them needs decontaminating. The most radioactive part of their bodies is their hair. They will all have to have their heads shaved. They had already sent for a barber.
Enter a medical assistant.

Assistant: I can't find any barbers sir.

Doctor: Why's that?

Assistant: They won't have anything to do with it.

Doctor: But cutting their hair off is the most vital step in the decontamination procedure.

Assistant: I know sir, but the barbers of Yaizu have, to a man, refused to have anything to do with the job. I'm afraid no barber in Yaizu can be found to cut the crewman's hair.

Doctor: All right, we'll have to do it ourselves

before transferring them to the hospital in Tokyo. Would you all come this way please?

The crewmen with their nurses, and the doctors, putting on rubber gloves, file out.
Kuboyama is the last to leave. He speaks to his wife.

Kuboyama: I'm not injured. They are only being careful. Anyway I drink too much. Now, don't worry about me. The hospital is good and I shall be all right. Take good care of the children.

He goes, leaving Mrs. Kuboyama alone, who, after a pause, goes in the opposite direction.
Silence.

Screen : **Controversy and Confusion**

Sound : 'The Stars and Stripes'.
The American flag.

American Congressman: Yes, I am the Republican Congressman from Pennsylvania, yes, and I am a member of the Joint Committee on Atomic Energy. And you want to know about the First of March H-bomb explosion. Well, that bomb equalled the blast of twelve to fourteen tons of TNT. I have been told that the bomb detonated from the top of the 150 foot tower on Bikini was a thousand times greater in power than the A-bomb which was first exploded over Hiroshima.

Sound : A Japanese temple gong.
A giant picture/silhouette/blow-up photograph of the Great Buddha at Kamakura.

Japanese Politician: This is incredible and terrible. As if we have not suffered enough already. A bomb a thousand times more destructive than the bomb dropped over our city of Hiroshima. It is impossible to imagine such violence packed within the confines of a single bomb.

An American secretary passes a note from the American area to the Japanese area. The Japanese politician reads it.

Japanese Politician: The United States have now established a new danger area. It encompasses about 400,000 square miles of territory—roughly eight times the area formed by the previously designated danger zone.

He rings a bell. Two Japanese appear with placard : MARITIME SAFETY BOARD OF JAPAN. *The Politician hands the two representatives the paper about enlargement of the danger zone. One of the Japanese speaks through a loud hailer.*

Politician: All fishing boats in this zone, or taking passage through it, are required to put into the following ports: Yaizu, Tokyo, Misaki, Shimizu, Shiogama to be inspected for signs of radio activity.

American Ambassador: I have been pleased to learn of the prompt action which has been taken by the Japanese and the American authorities to provide the most effective possible medical and technical assistance to those affected by the accident which befell the 'Lucky Dragon'.

Japanese Politician: We must assure the Japanese people that they are not being poisoned by the crying fish. We need the advice of our scientists.

Scientist appears with geiger counter.

Scientist: The problem is in determining a 'danger level' below which the fish can be considered harmless. Checking the external surfaces might not reveal internal contamination. Possibly the danger level may be set at 100 counts per minute for a geiger counter held at four inches from the fish.

Man from Safety Board: And the fish that pass the test should have a seal certifying them as free from dangerous radioactivity and therefore edible.

Scientist: I agree; we must take into account public ignorance and fear. The seal is a good idea, it will help to reassure them. *He goes.*

American Ambassador: Our joint investigations of the incident are already under

way and will I believe lead to findings, I am authorised to make clear that the US is prepared to take such steps as may be necessary to ensure fair and just compensation if the facts so warrant . . .

Gong

Japanese Politician: Facts so warrant? What does this mean? Is this diplomatic evasion? Does this mean there are doubts in the mind of the Americans about the injuries or the proximity of the 'Lucky Dragon' to the danger?

Enter two American Congressmen.

1st Congressman: I am a Congressman from Illinois and I wish to voice my concern; if the Japanese fishing boat got as close as it did to the blast indicated then a Soviet submarine could have pierced through the security precautions for a better vantage point.

2nd Congressman: This situation may also be interpreted to suggest that the 'Lucky Dragon' might have been on a spying mission. *They go.*

The gong reverberates as though angry.

Japanese Scientist: I don't think the Americans realise the serious condition the fishermen are in. It is my considered opinion as an atomic specialist that ten per cent of the 'Lucky Dragon' crew might die. I have kept this so far to myself lest it should shock the patients, but please remember that acute radiation disease is never to be belittled. Also it is difficult to estimate the amount of radiation the fishermen received. In spite of optimistic predictions we have no precedent in medical science for evaluating the impact of radiation which penetrated the whole body.

American area : Placard : SECRET MEETING.
Actors appear in dark clothes and hats acting conspiratorily. Each wears a label representing his organisation.
1. Food and Drug Administration
2. Atomic Energy Commission
3. State Department.

They collect together, whisper among themselves constantly assuring themselves that no-one is listening. They choose a spokesman, who remains disguised while he talks to the audience.

Spokesman: We have agreed on an acceptable level of radio-activity but we have classified this level as confidential and is not to be released to the public.

The conspirators stealthily disappear.

Placard : EXPORTER OF TUNA FISH *appears on the Japanese side. Placard :* AMERICAN IMPORTER *appears on American side.*

American Dealer: We should like to suspend shipments of frozen and canned tuna from Japan.

Japanese Dealer: But we've had a regular order from your company. We are already preparing the fish for shipment. You cannot simply suspend orders.

American Dealer: All right but all shipments must bear inspection certificates from the Ministry of Welfare.

Japanese Dealer: What level of radio-activity will you agree to accept. In Japan we believe that 100 counts per minute is safe, examined by geiger counter at the distance of four inches.

American Dealer: I'm afraid our stipulations will have to be more stringent. The fish must be examined at a distance closer than four inches, and there must be a detailed inspection of the gills. And the acceptable count level of a hundred may be all right for Japan, but it's certainly unacceptable by us. The count level must be much lower.

Japanese Dealer: I don't understand. Your Atomic Energy Commission tell us that there is no danger and you strongly imply that we are being unrealistic about radio-activity in fish. And now *you* are rejecting even *slightly* contaminated fish bound for consumption in the United States.

Placard : THE ATOMIC ENERGY COMMISSION

Chairman: The opinion of the Atomic Energy Commission scientific staff, based on long term studies of fish in the presence of radio-activity is that there is a negligible hazard, from the consumption of fish caught in the Pacific Ocean outside the immediate test area.

Gong.

Japanese Scientist: I have analysed the radio-active elements in the Bikini ash which add up to make Strontium 90 . . . The fish can have this radio-active substance in its body and yet not be detected from outside. Moreover, this Strontium 90 seeks out the bone tissues and once deposited there would live for a long time inside human beings, gradually destroying the bone structure. This radio activity we have detected is certainly not negligible.

Japanese Politician: Let's send the highly contaminated fish to the American Ambassador and have him eat it!

Placard : THE WHITE HOUSE, WASHINGTON, D.C.

Sound : The Stars and Stripes.

American Journalist: Mr. President: Some anti-American newspapers in Japan and other countries have seized on the 'Lucky Dragon' incident to make some very strong anti-American propaganda. I wonder if you would care to give us a statement of policy of the Government to the rest of the world in these tests.

The President: It was quite clear that this time something must have happened which we had never experienced before and must have surprised and astonished the scientists, and very properly the United States had to take precautions that had never occurred to them before.

Japanese housewife: I don't really understand all this radioactivity, as far as I'm concerned the fish is either radioactive or it's not. Either it is dangerous, or it is safe. I don't understand all this about 100 counts per minute. I buried the last lot of fish I bought, in the back yard . . .

Sound : The clicking of the geiger counter that increases in pace and rises to a high-pitched scream.

The American and the Japanese symbols disappear as the crew of the 'Lucky Dragon' are brought into the acting area helped by nurses and medical staff, some are on stretchers. Symbols of blood transfusion are set up.

Screen : **Hospital, Tokyo**

The medical staff murmur and repeat the word 'Reassurance'.

A large cut-out shape of a television screen; the actors are in three dimensions and act as puppets. The television set is apparently in the hospital ward. And we watch a 'mime show'.

Sound : percussion instruments, saucepan lids, wooden sticks, rattles, scrapers, bells and gongs accompany the action.

Action : A group of performers crouch as though like waves beneath an actor who is in a 'boat'. He is pulled along by the waves who suddenly stop and will go no further. The man in the boat tries to persuade the waves to take him further, the waves refuse to do so. They mime that they are approaching the Lord of the Sea's domain. The man states that he is not afraid, would they please continue. All right if the man in the boat insists. There is a strange sound, and, as though emerging from the sea, a giant, ferociously masked figure towers above the man in the boat and, to the rattling of percussion instruments, the man and the giant figure battle. The battle is a comic one with the man in the boat often getting the better of the Lord but quickly and deftly he swings a large black cloak that envelops the little man, and the waves lift the little man up struggling beneath the cloak.

The programme changes to street interviews and there is the collection of people, some trying to be seen by the camera, some being serious, some self-conscious.

Girl: I'm sure they'll lose weight.
Man: And all their bones will stick out like the victims of Hiroshima.
Girl: Isn't it true that they're going to die in six months?
Man: And that strange dust that fell on them, the papers are calling it Ashes of Death.
Girl: And isn't it true that the radio-activity makes you sterile?
Girl: I could never marry one of the 'Lucky Dragon' crewmen—we would never be able to have children.

The television is taken away. The medical staff continue to repeat 'reassurance'.

A journalist enters and reads from a newspaper
Screen : DOCTOR SAYS H-SICK MAY NOT WORK AGAIN.

Journalist: All the twenty-three Bikini blast-affected crewmen of the 'Lucky Dragon' are still in a serious condition despite recent reports to the contrary, Japanese doctors declared today. They say that although they have done all they could for the H-bomb dusted fishermen their condition shows no sign of improvement. The acute wasting away of the bone marrow will mean death in the long run.

A faint rhythm is heard. This rhythm develops and accompanies the action for the remainder of the play. During the next scenes the acting area slowly fills with people and decorations.
Screen : May 5, Boy's Day when large and colourful fish are flown throughout the land. A National Holiday.

The rhythm grows as people bring on large colourful fish on poles, together with balloons. The movement pauses. The rhythm becomes faint.

Screen : **May 18. Some of the fishermen, on road to recovery**

The rhythm grows again. The nurses lift their patients, except Kuboyama, to their feet and unbandage them and lead them out of the hospital area.
Screen : Kuboyama, the radio man of the 'Lucky Dragon' is taken to a private ward.
Kuboyama is taken by a nurse to a raised area, somewhere in the centre of the acting space.

Sound : The Stars and Stripes.
An American flag.
An American walks quickly into the acting area and announces :
American: The Series of Bomb Tests in the Pacific have been concluded. Military weapon test danger area limits disestablished.

The American and the flag make a quick exit.

Multicoloured 'fish' kites flown by Japanese children.

The rhythm grows and the area becomes a carnival with explosions of carnival flowers, wreaths of dazzling tinsel shimmering on poles, silver bubbles, stars, birds, fish, butterflies, garlands, an array of artificial decorations. People in motley dress, masked and painted faces, posters advertising variety shows, nude spectaculars. The rhythm builds to a great clash of cymbals . . . and a beautiful, ornate, colourful dragon appears attended by several devils and the Carnival procession develops into a game. 'He who touches the dragon will have one year added to his life but he who is touched by a devil will have one day deducted from his life.' *The game whirls with the dragon raising his grotesque head above the milling crowd. Unnoticed a black figure moves through the crowd to where Kuboyama lies. Mrs. Kuboyama is kneeling beside her husband. The movement of the Carnival comes to a standstill. The messenger waits until everyone is still.*

Messenger: Aikichi Kuboyama, fisherman and radio operator resident of Yaizu, Japan, died this evening at 6.57, September 23, 1954.

A nurse comes forward and places a white cloth over the body of Kuboyama.
In silence tapers are lit.

The American flag and the American Ambassador.

Ambassador: I have just been informed of the death of Aikichi Kuboyama, member of the crew of the 'Lucky Dragon'. I speak on behalf of the government and people of the United States in expressing extreme sorrow and regret at this most unhappy event . . .
No word of comfort can repair the loss of this man to his family, nothing can dispel the sorrow of his doctors who laboured so devotedly to save him, no action by his countrymen or mine can undo what has happened. In these respects and in many others too, we are as the Heike Monogatori truly says 'Only dust in the face of the wind'.

He goes. The American flag remains. The deep sound of a wooden bell tolls slowly. A girl picks up a mortuary tablet on which are written the words: 'The soul of the deceased Aikichi Kuboyama.'

Another girl carries a large photograph of Kuboyama. Mrs. Kuboyama carries the boxed urn containing the ashes of her husband. The procession moves off, led by the dragon and the devils. Mrs. Kuboyama is the last in the procession. An American stands by the American flag and as she moves past he says very quietly :

American: Mrs. Kuboyama.

She stops. She does not look at him.

American: We should like you to accept this as a token of sympathy of the American government and people.

He hands her a large piece of paper on which can be clearly seen written :
ONE MILLION YEN.
She takes it without acknowledgement. He goes.
We see a woman with the urn of her husband's ashes in one hand and in the other holding a cheque for a million yen. The procession has since gone. We hear the faint echoes of the wooden bell. Mrs. Kuboyama follows the direction of the sound.

Screen : **Aikichi Kuboyama**

Cause of Death
Intensive disorder of the liver due to:
1. Serum heptitus, caused by blood transfusion, or
2. degeneration of the liver caused by debris of other radio sensitive cells destroyed by radiation injury, or
3. primary radiation injury, or
4. ,all the factors in combination.

Some plays

a. Classical plays
The Government Inspector
Oedipus the King
Fuente Ovejuna
Coriolanus

b. Contemporary plays
Mother Courage
Serjeant Musgrave's Dance

a. Classical plays

The world of established drama is rich in rewarding material. The notes that follow are necessarily only fragments, suggesting areas to explore rather than complete statements on the plays.

The four plays themselves were chosen to represent certain differing styles of presentation and periods of drama, leading to other areas of exploration.

Nobody can lay down rules about how plays should be presented. There are a variety of interpretations and approaches. These notes are suggestions of some avenues that might be explored.

The Government Inspector, Theatre Workshop.

The Government Inspector by Nicholai Gogol
Russia 1835

Gogol's *The Government Inspector* (or *The Inspector General*) is a comedy which pokes savage fun at the hypocrisy of small town officials, of petty government employees and tiny-minded men in power. The 'Government Inspector' himself is an impoverished clerk who lands in a small town in nineteenth-century Russia, and is mistaken for a visiting government inspector from St. Petersburg—the capital. The impostor revels in his assumed role, and in doing so exposes a whole set of phoney people who hilariously play up to him.

Such is the power of the satire that, when it was first performed, the government officials of the day immediately recognised the truth of the statements, and raised an outcry against the play and the author.

At the time of its performance, plays in the mode of the French playwright *Moliere* were in vogue in St. Petersburg, and the play is cast in the mould of a classic comedy. It is in five acts, reflects exactly the social hierarchy of a family and of a small community and is concerned with the intrigues within the family and the community.

The characters are, however, individuals as distinctive and unique to Gogol as Dickens's characters are to him. They are people of extraordinarily rich idiosyncrasies—they are in earnest, and yet are shamefully comic. The Mayor is a sort of grotesque puppet, but he is also a reflection of much that is ourselves—a reflection of a real Mayor. 'What are you laughing at?', he says to us, 'You are laughing at yourselves'.

Gogol was unhappy with the way in which the actors first interpreted his lines and wrote detailed notes on the characters, which are usually printed with the text.

The play

It is essentially about a Russian society which has almost disappeared. It is a feudal peasant society with fear and respect for aristocratic ideas. The town officials are peasants in feeling, but middle class in behaviour and custom. They are full of self-importance, and shake in front of the supposed upper class official. But they are peasants just below the surface. Agriculture, fields, farms, muddy streets, wooden shacks and houses, snow and cold, genteel poverty—these are lurking around the edges of the play. It is not fancy dress 'Ruritania', but reality, without trains, drains, electricity; a cut-off town miles from anywhere.

Such towns are sometimes seen in Western films, and they can be found, at certain times of the year in remote parts of England.

The attitudes expressed are current now. Any official inspection, even on a very humble level, produces a similar display of role-playing and grovelling. It is, therefore, very much about people as they still appear today.

Staging and rehearsing

1. Read the play through several times, to get knowledge of the action and the characters, and a feeling for the structure of the play. Try to understand the development and at what points key ideas are introduced. As a starting point, consider these moments from Act One:

(i) *A room in the Mayor's house*

The first speech sets the whole play moving:

> I have asked you to come to see me, gentlemen, because I have a very unpleasant piece of news to communicate to you. We're going to have a visit from a Government Inspector.

The whole action depends upon this news and the effect on those gathered to hear it.

Find out what that effect is, and who the people are who hear it. Then examine the place and the people, one by one. What are their characteristics and how do they fit into the whole?

Write biographies of each character, and discuss them with the rest of the group.

(ii) From this develops the reality of the situation—what the inspector will find, and how terrified they are of him.

(iii) *Bobchinsky and Dobchinsky come in breathless with running.*

Bob: A most extraordinary thing!
Dob: An unexpected piece of news!

there follows a scene of excited and confused interchange—in the course of which they say that they visited an inn.

Bob: But no sooner had we walked into the inn than a young man suddenly.

Dob: Quite good looking, but in civilian clothes—

Bob: Quite good looking, but in civilian clothes—

(The idea of a visitor is planted)

(The interchange continues until—)

Bob: Yes, sir. Well you see he is that official.

The archetypal comedy situation of wrong identity—Bobchinsky and Dobchinsky have chosen the wrong man.

(iv) Panic. Revelations about the corrupt and social evils in the running of the town.

(v) Introduction of the Mayor's wife and daughter.

Wife: What has he come, the Government Inspector? Has he a moustache? What sort of moustache?

2. Comedy: This is basic comedy material, based, like early Chaplin, in a social setting. It relies very much on verbal wit, like the Marx Brothers. It has an emphasis on exaggerated characters like a pantomime, but is rigidly controlled. Try:

(a) Playing a scene in an invented language. The characters communicate but do not understand the words being used.

(b) Using gibberish but still communicating between the actors.

(c) Speeding the action up, and then slowing it down.

(d) Singing the dialogue, as it were in opera.

Remember: The basis of the performance is concentration. Ask yourself, *who* is this character. Am I being true to how he would act?

Where is it taking place? What is the nature of the environment? Is it true to the atmosphere of the play?

What is happening? Is it clear? Is the action developing along the lines laid down by the author? Don't try to make the play funny. It is funny as it is. Play it as it stands.

Costumes: The play provides a real opportunity for expressing cartoon-like characteristics in terms of the costumes worn.

Make-up: Make-up is really an extension of the mask. Its main purpose is to reinforce the actor's interpretation. It can emphasise features, but it *can* work totally against them.

3. *Situations:* It greatly helps understanding of sections and individual scenes if they are examined in relation to current situations.

(a) Consider a scene in which, for example, somebody was expected (an aunt from Australia, a sister's boy friend). A completely different person arrives and finds he is treated as the expected visitor. How does everybody react?

(b) The headmaster inspects the books of the class. The teacher hasn't been teaching correctly (or hasn't done the marking). The boys haven't done the work properly.

(c) A queen is due to open a public building. Somebody else is mistaken for her. What happens when the queen finally arrives?

(d) A 'wild west' town. The inhabitants are waiting for a travelling judge. They mistake a travelling salesman for the judge.

The finding of such situations helps the understanding of the original situation and gives the performance more bite.

4. *Characters:* Here are some of the things Gogol says about the characters:

The Mayor—in his own opinion far from stupid—talks neither too much nor too little—features hard and rough—coarsely developed instinct—wears uniform and boots—greying short hair.

His Wife—provincial coquette—curious and vain—reads albums and novels—changes her clothes four times.

Khlestakov—23, thin—slender—stupid 'ninny'—speech abrupt—dressed fashionably.

Osip—serious—looks on the ground when talking—voice smooth—severe and churlish expression—more intelligent than his master—a taciturn rascal—wears a shabby grey or blue coat.

Bobchinsky and Dobchinsky—shortish little men, very inquisitive—talk rapidly—gesticulate a great deal.

Each of these statements (and the others used by Gogol) contain seeds of possible studies of a range of characteristics, types and human foibles. Study the phrases used by Gogol and base an examination of different people on them. In pairs take different words and together explore their effect (e.g. thin—simplehearted). As a group build up a complete picture of the types you imagine the characters in the play to be.

Oedipus the King by Sophocles
Greece 425 BC

The play

Oedipus is an ancient Greek play which asks the questions 'What is life?' and 'Who controls it?'. Oedipus, believes he can control life and sets out to prove it.

He is a young king of Thebes. Iocasta, the Queen, is older. She was previously married to King Laius, who was killed by robbers, it is said, whilst out on a journey. Some time later Oedipus, a stranger, arrived at Thebes from a distant land.

Thebes at that time was under the siege of the terrible sphinx, a creature able to cast cruel spells, and Oedipus, on his arrival, was able to solve the riddle of the sphinx and rid the Thebans of her curse. For such deliverance the people begged him to be their king, and Iocasta accepted him as husband.

At the time the play starts Oedipus is well established as the king. Thebes once again is in the grip of a curse, this one worse than the sphinx. The plague has swept the city, people die in misery and horror—the city

'is now,
Storm-tossed, and can no longer raise its head
Above the waves and angry surge of death.'

The people come to ask Oedipus to help them again in their trouble, and the King has sent to the oracle at Delphi to learn the cause of the city's oppression. The Queen's brother returns with the message from the oracle.

'There is pollution
Here in our midst, long-standing. This must we
Expel, nor let it grow past remedy.'

He reveals that the murderer of King Laius is here in their midst, and death, plague and torment will grow in the city until the killer is routed out and punished.

Oedipus appoints himself the person to uncover the identity of the killer, and sets about examining the evidence and detecting the whereabouts of the assassin.

'I will begin again, I'll find the truth.'

Systematically he starts an enquiry.

He learns that King Laius had a son, and that

son, it was prophesied, would kill him. Because of the prophesy, the baby was taken away, up into the mountains, to be killed. He learns that the son was not in fact killed, but first tended by a shepherd who later gave the baby to a shepherd from another land, for fear the deception be discovered by King Laius. This child was never heard of again, but he did live, and he did have the opportunity of killing his father.

Who was it then, who killed the King when he was out journeying? Oedipus's questioning is so ruthless and penetrating that he cannot escape the truth, and is indeed, in spite of many warnings, determined not to. For Oedipus discovers that *he*, the stranger, is the killer. An old traveller entangled with him at some crossroads—this was King Laius. Why was Oedipus travelling himself? Because the oracle had also said that he was doomed to kill his own father and marry his mother. And Oedipus, knowing nothing of his origins, believing himself to be the son of a noble in Corinth—given to the childless pair by the shepherd—had run away from his 'father' and 'mother', to Thebes, as he thought a strange land.

The detective discovers the murderer. It is himself.

Iocasta, the Queen, runs away and hides. She is discovered hanging. Oedipus takes the clasps from her brooches, stabs them in his eyes, and blinds himself. He is led, stumbling from the city —thus ridding it of its plagues and troubles.

The play in performance

The action of the play happens on the steps of the palace and the square before it, in one continuous action. It has speeches, broken by song and dance, yet the whole has a solemnity properly belonging to a religious ceremony.

Originally the play would have been performed at the festival of Dionysus, the God of Drama, in Athens. On the first day of the festival a magnificent procession would wind through the city to a shrine, where a bull was sacrificed to the image of the god. After dark, the image was taken to the theatre, amid a torchlight procession. The festival lasted five days—during which plays were performed in competition.

Each morning at dawn a purification ceremony was performed, with the priest of Dionysus at the centre of the theatre. Behind him spread a vast audience of up to seventeen thousand people. The

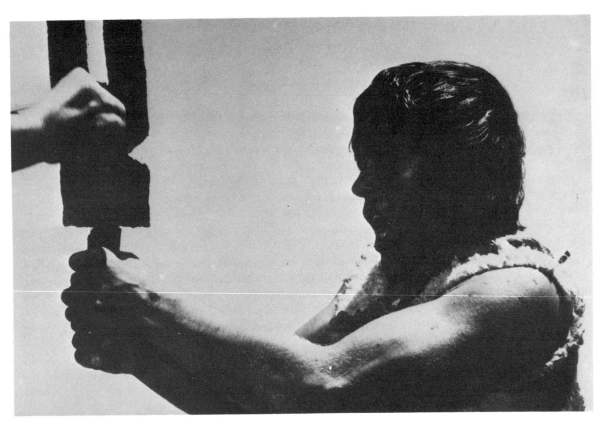

Film still: 'Oedipus Rex' directed by Pasolini.

whole city stopped work for the festival. The theatre was open to the sky, on a hillside, overlooking the sea and the city. The audience sat on the slope of the hill, looking down on the arena. This was a large stage, circular, about sixty feet in diameter. Towards the back of this was a long, low, wooden hall, with a large central door and a platform before it. The chorus spoke and danced in the arena, the actors on the platform. The actors wore masks, richly coloured robes and decorated shoes. The masks, made of linen and cork, were large and painted with the expressions of the character. The voices used were controlled and stylised, and the movements precise.

Modern performances can rarely recapture this setting and method of presentation, and the religious aspect of the play has no meaning today. Certain aspects of the original presentation can be re-envisaged in present-day terms, both in the actual content of the story, and in methods of presentation.

Areas of Exploration

1. Improvisation

(i) *Oedipus the King* is an ancient ceremonial play. It contains a strong ritualistic element. Explore the idea of a ceremony for praising the God of Drama. Invent a coronation for Oedipus.

Suggest a method for the people to approach the King on the steps of the palace begging for his help in their trouble. Develop movements which have strong rhythms, for the people, and for the king and the queen.

(ii) Take the idea of a prophesy—this is an extension of the religious and ritualistic aspects of the play. Explore how people react to a prophesy.

Take the prophesy that Laius's son will kill him. Improvise on this. The king and queen agree to have the baby killed—he is taken to the mountains, a boulder attached to his foot, and he is left to die. A passing shepherd hears the cries and runs towards the baby. Apart from a smashed foot (the meaning of the word Oedipus), the baby's life is saved.

The shepherd looks after it. Fear of death from the king leads him to give the child to another shepherd from Corinth. The king of Corinth is childless and hearing of this boy adopts him as his heir. Oedipus grows up believing this.

(iii) Oedipus goes to the oracle at Delphi. A vast

open space, with crowds of people demanding to know the future.

Oedipus learns that one day he will kill his father and marry his mother. Horrified he decides to go as far away from Corinth as he can. He goes in the other direction, to Thebes.

(iv) On his journey he comes to a crossroads. There he sees an old man and some servants. They order him out of the way, and hit him with sticks. Oedipus rounds on them, and kills the old man. He continues his journey.

(v) He arrives at the mourning city of Thebes, guarded by the hideous sphinx, half animal, half woman, a creature of great magical power. If a passer-by cannot answer her riddle, the sphinx leaps upon the traveller and kills him. Oedipus is asked the riddle, which is: 'What animal goes about in the morning on four feet, in the afternoon on two feet and in the evening on three?'

Oedipus answers—'Man. In the morning of his life he crawls on feet and hands. In his middle-life he walks on two feet, and when he is old he needs a stick—thus three feet!'. The sphinx is defeated.

(vi) Celebrations. The people are overjoyed. There is much singing, dancing and drinking of wine.

The news of Laius's death reaches the city. Mourning takes over. Oedipus is asked to become king. He agrees.

(vii) Coronation. Oedipus the King. Iocasta the Queen.

2 Exploring themes

(i) Explore dramatically a variety of interpretations and associations of such ideas as 'Kingship', 'murderer', 'marriage'.

(ii) Explore dance rhythms and movements suggested by such things as 'plague', 'holiday', 'horror', 'jubilation'.

(iii) Explore sounds and incantations for the various elements in the play.

(iv) Examine the role of the gods, of fate. Discuss the element of prediction in life. How much faith do people have in horoscopes, astrologers, fortune tellers?

(v) Consider the idea of a city as an extension of a man. What is necessary today to make a satisfactory city? To what extent can the king in the play be regarded as the centre of the city? Therefore is the play about the unsuitability of the king and the need to get rid of him, for the good of the city? Or is it about one man's particular problems and destiny?

3. Masks and costumes

Devise imaginative masks for Oedipus, Iocasta, the Sphinx, the people (and other characters, Tiresias—the blind seer, Creon the brother-in-law).

Invent and make simple costumes in strong colours with bold designs.

4. The text

Oedipus the King is a tightly constructed play. It is, however, enormously difficult to act. The part of Oedipus is an exhausting one. The story, on the other hand, is a rich and rewarding one, and there is every reason for using it as a basis for drama work. Sections of the play could be used and adapted, or abandoned altogether, depending on the group's understanding of the language and on their ability to cope with the text.

5. Space

The approach suggested would require a large, open space. It would mean the use of expansive sound, masks, costume and plenty of light. The open air is appropriate, but not often convenient. The floor of a hall, rather than a stage, with the audience surrounding the action, rather than looking up at it is more in keeping with the play.

Reference books

Drama in Performance Raymond Williams
Greek Drama H. D. Kitto

Other plays of interest

Antigone, Oedipus at Colonus by Sophocles
Plays by Aeschylus, Aristophanes

Fuente Ovejuna by Lope de Vega
Spain 1614

Lope de Vega was born in 1562, two years before Shakespeare. He is reputed to have written about 1,700 plays.

The play

Fuente Ovejuna is the name of a village, which still exists in Spain, and means 'sheep's well'. In the fifteenth century, when the play is set, it was a small farming village. In 1476, Spain (the Iberian peninsula) was wracked with internal politics. The play is about a war between Ferdinand and Isabella of Aragon in the North of Spain, and Alfonso, King of Portugal, over the possession of Castille in the centre of Spain.

In 1476 known civilisation was centred on the Mediterranean Sea. Scholars were aware that the earth might be a sphere—popular belief was that it was flat, and small. The world was made up of small states with kings who ruled by the divine will of God, and who relied on the qualification of blood relationship to take over the throne from a father or an uncle.

The known lands (known that is to the writers and historians who recorded the life of people in 1476) were large masses of land such as Gaul, Iberia, Italy, which were composed of states ruled over by dukes, princes, kings and queens, jostling with each other to gain more land, wealth, prestige and information. Ideas spread, people travelled, armies were formed, battles fought, fleets manned and religion flourished. There was much confusion—transport and communications were poor. The nature of the universe, the extent of its territory, the peoples it contained were largely unknown. It was 16 years before Ferdinand and Isabella were to finance Columbus on his voyages.

In this world, war, plague, riches, God, the elements, rival claims to states and cities, survival, ignorance, jostled with each other. Titles, wealth and uncertain boundaries led to never-ending battles between states. Wars with the African races were frequent. The Moors invaded Portugal, Andalucia, Castille, Granada. The city of Cuidad Real, plumb in the middle of Spain was a key point. Alfonso claimed it, Ferdinand and Isabella claimed it, and they both had sound reasons. It commanded the best strategic point for controlling the whole of Spain. In 1476 they fought bloodily.

Fuente Ovejuna stands to the south of Cuidad Real, and the villagers were typical of all villagers in a feudal society. They could not read or write. To them the world ended, practically, at the village boundary. Their king was their ultimate master next to God. Their own immediate master, the Lord of the Manor, lived in the village, he was a soldier and a nobleman, Fernan Gomez de Guzman. They worked in the fields and produced food to keep themselves and their master alive. Their spokesman was the Mayor, Estaban, who ran the village in its day-to-day life. The others worked the farms, tended the sheep and generally lived a peaceful and quiet life. The wars going on between princes and kings were nothing to do with them. Guzman would sometimes march off at the head of a column of men, and they would not see him until he returned. Guzman was a Commander in the Order of the Knights of Calatrava. He was an unpleasant man, and the villagers were pleased to see him go, especially the women, for the Commander treated the women very badly.

So, in 1476, the villagers were pleased to see him ride off with his henchmen, Ortuno and Flores, to fight in the battle for Cuidad Real. The Commander was to side with Portugal, and Portugal was to lose the battle. The villagers enjoyed the peace during the Commander's absence. Laurencia, the Mayor's daughter, and Frondoso her fiance planned to marry during this time, because Frondoso was a marked man by the Commander. But the Commander, defeated, returned to Fuente Ovejuna, and took vengeance on the villagers. He arrived in the course of the wedding feast, and seized Laurencia, taking her off to his castle. The villagers were horrified and outraged, for the Commander had broken the strong code of honour under which they all lived. When Laurencia returned to them, bloody and bruised, they decided to seek vengeance.

They marched on the castle, ransacked it and killed the Commander and one of his henchmen. The other escaped to take the news to Ferdinand —the victor of Cuidad Real. Under the feudal law, whoever killed the Commander was guilty, and the King sent a judge, a member of the

All citizens are soldiers (Fuente Ovejuna) Contemporary Theatre.

infamous inquisition, to find out the killer. He took with him the rack, and each villager in turn was tortured on it, but in answer to the question: 'Who killed the Commander?', each person said 'Fuente Ovejuna'—i.e. the whole village killed him. The judge returned with the verdict that the whole village was guilty. The villagers explained to the King and Queen the circumstances, and they were forgiven.

The structure of the play and the characters

The play divides clearly into three areas, and in each category there is a wealth of character.

(i) *The Court*
The court was the centre of power, wealth and patronage. It was a time of discovery, court intrigues, a taste in art and architecture, court preparations for war, involvement in religion (the Pope at this time was Spanish). Above all,

Ferdinand and Isabella, whatever they were in real life, stand in the play for positive moral values. They are seen to be just rulers, and it is around them that the action revolves. They represent the ultimate good—the representatives of God. Therefore order, justice and honour rest on them at the centre, radiating moral and spiritual values.

The visual splendour of the court was magnificent, and a strong contrast to the peasant element.

(ii) *The Order of the Knights of Calatrava*
All who challenge this centre must be defeated by it. The Commander is at the opposite extreme. Lustful, greedy, revengeful, immoral, dishonourable—he is the epitome of human degradation, the villain, who, like the devil, tries to destroy the balance of human goodness. He is gigantic in his wickedness—to challenge the power of God he must be powerful and arrogant, fearsome and

overpowering. These qualities fill the villagers with fear. His henchmen, like bodyguards to a gangster, are vicious and frightening.

The Master of Calatrava is the Commander's superior, a much younger man, little more than a boy, who is manipulated by the Commander. As long as he opposes the King and Queen he is weak and defeated. When he admits his mistakes, he is forgiven, and becomes strong.

(iii) *The villagers of Fuente Ovejuna*
Socially at the bottom of the ladder, the entire village form part of the base of the order on which the society was structured. The people work to maintain that order, of which Isabella and Ferdinand are the pinnacle. Thus the essential goodness of the village is part of the harmony of the whole. The honour of the villagers is the code of the society. Fuente Ovejuna is a haven of peace and restfulness.

Within the small world of the village people likewise have their places. Estaban, the mayor, is the pinnacle of the order of the village—the echo of the King, and therefore the opposite of the Commander. Laurencia, his daughter, is an extension of him, and therefore the most holy object to be grasped by the devilish Commander. The other villagers range around these two, making a solid representation of positive values. Mengo and Frondoso, Pascuela and Jacinta, add in an ingredient of humanity, making the village a place full of fun and humanity, warmth and joy, strength and honour.

The scheme of the play is a classic confrontation between good (the villagers of Fuente Ovejuna) and bad (the Commander) balanced by the existence of divine order (the King). The pendulum swings between the two extremes, but always from a central point. It is a play of great simplicity —quite coolly based on the belief that although man will suffer much, good will triumph in the end.

Areas of Exploration

1. *Scenes of action*
Explore these and exploit them for their dramatic worth. Soldiers dragging off villagers, the battle, the wedding feast, the sacking of the castle, the torturing on the rack—these should be controlled but spectacular.

2. *Historical background*
Cassell's book *Ferdinand and Isabella* gives a very clear idea of the sumptuous quality of the court, the ferociousness of the wars, the intense religious feeling, and the appearance of the life of the peasants. It would be useful to make a folder containing a collection of maps, paintings, and facts about the period.

3. *The argument*
Consider: (i) The passionate sincerity of the peasants. Recreate scenes from the life of the village. Improvise dances and village scenes— working in the field, meeting in the village, at home in the cottages.
(ii) The arrogant violence of the commander. Introduce the conflict that this produces. Recreate scenes in the castle, in the army.
(iii) The rightness of the King and Queen. Explore aspects of the court. Improvise scenes in which the King and Queen organise their kingdom and their subjects.

4. *Staging*
This must, from the point of economics, be kept simple. Refer to pictures of the time, but find simple methods of expressing the basic difference between the three groups—they must be kept clear. Avoid too much 'fancy-touristy Spanish' effects.

All citizens are soldiers

An interesting version of the play has been prepared by Alan Sillitoe and Ruth Fainlight. They have seen in the play a reflection of the struggles in twentieth-century Spain, and have added a prologue set in Madrid in 1936 in the Spanish Civil War.

Soldiers resting from a hard time at the front have taken over an old theatre as a billet. They number among them wounded and fatigued soldiers. The manager of the theatre, keen to take advantage of the incoming 'audience', prepares to entertain the soldiers with a suitable play. The play, *Fuente Ovejuna*, has certain affinities with their own situation, and will guide them in what is going on.

Songs are added, the soldiers themselves joining in, some playing parts, some making comments. Since the play in Lope de Vega's time would have been performed in the open air, in a courtyard with balconies looking over the acting space, the idea of the audience mixed in with the action, looking down and commenting, is very much in keeping with the style of Lope's play.

The music should be original settings of the songs or traditional Spanish ballads adapted, to suit such songs as:

> Brother and son
> Uncle and father
> Take up your swords
> To kill each other :
> We're off to the war
> Between sun and moon :
> But we know whose blood
> Will be flowing soon
> We're off to the war
> Between fire and water
> Close up your ranks
> And call it slaughter :
> The river flows red
> From Iberia's daughter.
> Brother and son
> And brother and brother
> Take up your guns
> To kill each other.

The central play is the same as in Lope de Vega. The adaptation is in a colloquial style. The ending is slightly different. Whereas the peasants are forgiven for the death of the tyrant, and the village taken under the protection of Ferdinand and Isabella in the original—in this version they are forgiven and then pressed into service to fight the enemy. The peasants lose out to their feudal superiors. *All Citizens Are Soldiers* ends with the 1936 war breaking in: 'Everybody to the front'.

> No sleep tonight, no sleep.
> Rest is for the sky, not us.
> Not even stone or concrete
> Or dead metal. No sleep
> For hands, no sleep for guns.
> Only death and bullets.
> Skulls and the death rattle.
> No sleep for eyes that want to close,
> No sleep tonight, no sleep
> For them nor us. The night
> Is running out of breath
> No sleep in this long fight with death.

Mengo: Death to the Moors! Death to the fascists!

They are running out—the crowd on stage is thinning, Mengo is guiding them, exhorting. Sirens, explosions, marching feet. They are singing outside as they march off.

Curtain remains up as the audience leaves the theatre. A loudspeaker is blaring a political speech in Spanish over their heads. The stage is empty.
END END END

The Spanish Civil War was a complex affair, difficult to summarise, difficult to untangle. The struggle between Crown and people, Church and Army, confused the Spaniards themselves and sympathisers from outside. It was a bloody struggle. In November 1936, Fascist forces, led by Franco, heavily bombed the population of Madrid, and a beginning was made to a long and exhausting siege of the capital, which was at the time in the hands of the Republicans, who were democratically elected. Franco eventually won. It is to the Republicans that the Sillitoe version of *Fuente Ovejuna* is addressed.

To approach the play from this angle may give it an added interest, leading to a separate study of the Spanish Civil War. The civil war would make a giant subject for a project, and the study of it would underline some of the points in the Lope de Vega play, making them seem more relevant to a modern audience.

Reference books

Fuente Ovejuna translated Jill Boty
All Citizens Are Soldiers Ruth Fainlight and Alan Sillitoe, Macmillan
Ferdinand and Isabella published Cassell
The Spanish Civil War Hugh Thomas, Penguin
Homage to Catalonia George Orwell, Secker & Warburg

Record
Songs from the Spanish Civil War Folkways

Film
To Die in Madrid

Coriolanus by William Shakespeare
England 1608

All of Shakespeare's plays are rich minefields; rich in theme, character and situation and are ready to be explored and plundered. However, approaching a Shakespeare play can be thwart with problems, especially the problem of language. Shakespeare wrote in the sixteenth and seventeenth centuries and his vocabulary, although rich, heightened and dramatic, and charged with meaning, is often unfamiliar and not always immediately comprehensible. This should not be a deterrent. Shakespeare wrote his plays to be acted and even introducing elements of movement while reading with book in hand will help to bring the script alive and give meaning to the dialogue.

It is useful, once the motivation of the characters is understood within the given situation, to improvise the dialogue before trying to learn the script. Refer constantly to the text and try to define unfamiliar words. The outline here is a suggested approach to *Coriolanus*—it is not the only approach but some of the methods suggested may be adapted and applied to other plays.

Background

Elizabeth I is dead. There is a dearth of corn in England. Revolt breaks out in the Midlands. There is a gradual and continual rise in prices. The play expresses the people's dissatisfaction with the country's leadership and the development of a community from a monarchy to a constitutional republic. The two tribunes, the representatives of the people, in the play act like Jacobean City Magistrates. The play is as much about the people of London of Shakespeare's time as it is about the people of ancient Rome. Factions faced each other in the streets of London in very much the same way as the plebeians and the patricians face each other in the streets of Rome. The arguments are public brawls. Violent politics is the meat of the play. The Puritans tried to shut down the theatre as a breeding place of sin and pestilence. The Catholics tried to blow up the predominantly Puritan Parlia-

ment. In 1607 peasants revolted because of the confiscation by the nobles of communally held lands. Oliver Cromwell was nine years old, and forty years later England was to be plunged into Civil War and a King was to be publicly executed.

Not only did Shakespeare read a translation of *Plutarch's Lives* but he also looked and listened to what was going on in the streets of London. The play reflects in some respects the rise of the artisans, and the common people influencing the politics of the time. Shakespeare chose to symbolise the events of his time in an ancient story that took place around 490 BC when Rome was not yet an Imperial state under the Caesars but a relatively small, self-contained barbaric city. Therefore the play's background operates at two levels: London, five years after the death of Elizabeth I, and the barbaric state of Rome nearly 500 years before the birth of Christ.

The play

Coriolanus opens with the people of Rome in open mutiny, brandishing pikes, staves, clubs and weapons. There is famine in Rome and the citizens are resolved to die rather than famish. The patricians own the corn stores and among them is Caius Martius the notorious enemy of the people. The plebeians demand a reduction in the price of grain to one they can afford. Martius does not agree; he would let them die like rats or quarter them with his sword. The argument is interrupted by news of an advancing army of Volsces. Martius welcomes the news of war; the plebeians are war scarred; it is not the first time Rome has been to war; and the patricians who have grown rich on war cannot carry through a battle without the plebeians. Caius Martius is appointed a commander and the men of the city are immediately conscripted and drummed towards the battlefield. The battle between the Romans and the Volsces takes place in and around Corioles. Here Caius Martius proves himself to be a superb soldier, winning, almost single handed a victory for Rome. The plebeians on the other hand prove to be cowards and plunderers. To cheering troops Caius Martius is awarded the title of Coriolanus.

Coriolanus returns to Rome in triumph, rapturously greeted by the formerly hostile plebeians. He had saved them from pillage, slavery and destruction. However he continues to revile and

Coriolanus played on planks and scaffolding by students of N. Buckinghamshire College of Education.

insult them. The patricians nominate Coriolanus for the office of Consul, for which he needs the approval of the people. His election is blocked by the chicanery and intrigues of the two Tribunes who had been appointed earlier to appease the people and were their representatives participating in the governing of Rome. They accuse Coriolanus of plotting against the State. The antagonism of Act I revives. The vituperation of Coriolanus provokes violence, Coriolanus must stand trial. The patricians are unable to defend him against the plotting and manipulation of the people by the Tribunes. The plebeians force

Coriolanus to be banished. He escapes with the howls of the pursuing mob in his ears.

Coriolanus enters Antium, the city of the Volsces, disguised as a refugee, wary of being recognised and attacked. However, he manages to persuade Tullus Aufidius, the Volscian commander, to advance upon Rome. This collaboration promises to be advantageous to the Volscians in helping Coriolanus to take revenge upon his native city. Coriolanus assumes command of the Volscian forces, thus incurring the jealousy of Aufidius. Rome, which had become more relaxed since the banishment of Coriolanus suddenly becomes panic-stricken. It has exiled its greatest warrior and now he has turned against them, leading an army to destroy and enslave them. Rome feels powerless and vunerable realising that they could not resist the impending on-slaught. They try to appease him and beg for mercy. Coriolanus is adamant. The plebeians and the patricians accuse each other. Finally, they send his mother, his wife and his child to entreat him not to destroy his home and his family. Coriolanus agrees to make peace and retreats with the Volscian army away from the gates of Rome. He is now a traitor to his allies. He is publicly assassinated.

Throughout the play, five basic conflicts are played out:

(i) The plebeians, the poor, versus the patricians, the rich.
(ii) Rome versus her enemy, the Volscians.
(iii) Coriolanus versus the Volscian general, Tullus Aufidius.
(iv) Coriolanus versus his mother.
(v) The struggle within Coriolanus himself.

The characters

Coriolanus is an honest, super soldier but no politician. When the plebeians riot he would put them down with force. What he says of the people is perfectly true but the manner in which he says it is arrogant and provocative. He despises the common people. He is a product of his culture, his inherited position and the influence of his mother. She taught him to suppress all tenderness and love, and that winning in the manly pastime of killing in battle was the way to her heart. The people hate him. Their hatred is returned. Valiant in battle, incompetent at personal rela-tionships, he is entirely without cunning or guile. He is also exceedingly brave and selfless. He has been wounded twenty-seven times in his service to Rome; he captures Corioli, and yet does not want his share of the booty. Also he would rather not talk about his heroic deeds, they embarrass him. Neither does he want others to talk about them.

Coriolanus is: chief enemy of the people, very dog to the commonality, proud, a hunter, noble, de-voured by war, insolent, famous, a traitor, patriotic, he makes his enemies shake, he loves the smell of blood, he is a war machine, he forgets the name of the man who helped him, he is the devil, he does not care whether he has the people's love or not, his sword was death's stamp, he was a thing of blood, he struck Corioles like a planet, he looked upon the spoils of war as though they were muck, a tyrant, a foe of the public weal, he is a disease that must be cut away, he is too abso-lute . . .

> Though in this city he
> Hath widowed and unchilded many a one,
> Which to this hour bewail the injury,
> Yet he shall have a noble memory.

Menenius is the experienced politician, a clever manipulator of words; it is he who, through his fable of the state being like the body, is able to divert the crowd from their intention of murder-ing Caius Martius. He also is a patrician and a tactician, seeing things always from the patri-cian's point of view. He is a practical reasoner.

Tullus Aufidius is the leader of the Volsces. He is the Volscian lion in whom Coriolanus has a great respect. Coriolanus states that if he were not Coriolanus he would most like to be Tullus Aufidius. Aufidius is neither as noble nor as honourable as Coriolanus. He plots the assassina-tion of Coriolanus before he knows that Corio-lanus has decided to retreat. Nevertheless, he is a great warrior who likens himself to Achilles and Coriolanus to Hector, the superhuman legendary warriors.

Volumnia the mother of Coriolanus who has been described as a 'blood-mad eccentric' wields the strongest influence over her son and is perhaps an even tougher political manipulator than Menen-ius. She has great pride in her son's achievements, and recounts with relish that when she had sent Coriolanus to war as a comely youth, he returned the victor, and she was proud of his glory. She has obviously done much to shape her son's life.

The Tribunes, Sicinius and Brutus, have an aptitude for political manipulation. Together they prove more adroit than Menenius. We see them plot, step by step the banishment of Coriolanus. In modern terms they may be likened to shop stewards who know the way of the world and what makes the common man tick; they are the people's representatives who strive to serve the people. They see—quite rightly—Coriolanus as a threat to the State's well-being and their own new-won authority.

The Plebeians are the people who crowd the streets. These include a mixture of beggars, wastrels, vagabonds, clowns, cobblers, washer-women, orange sellers, botchers (old clothes menders), bakers, wheelwrights, blacksmiths . . .

According to Coriolanus the plebeians are: curs, scabs, geese, rabble fragments, rats, mutineers, base slaves, filthy, they feed on one another, mutable, rank-scented, measles, crows, common cry of curs, a hydra-headed monster . . .

The setting

Coriolanus is set in city streets, public places and battlefields. There are only two small domestic interior scenes: the kitchens of a Volscian banqueting hall and a room in Volumnia's house. City images blend with war images; the world of *Coriolanus* is hard and metallic. The images are hard: *leaden pounds, manacles, irons of doit, cushions of flint, hunger breaks stone walls, temples will be burned in their cement.* The environment is without comfort. The cities are surrounded by walls and the only entrance is through giant gates. The walls suggest communities who are afraid of marauding enemies; of burning lights at night surrounded by acres of darkness. Cities where the citizens can clamber on walls to see their hero, where stalls, bulks, windows, leads, ridges can be crowded with people. A set made of builder's scaffolding, with planks and ladders will perhaps suggest a location that can be walls and houses.

The language

In the play the language is unromantic, the images and the words match the action. Do not get caught up in the words; the phrasing and subtleties, the complexities and the levels of meaning can be fascinating but too much study can prevent action. Each time you return to a Shakespeare play you will discover something new. It must be recognised that the words are the starting point for action. Initially, aim to make the story clear. All 'plot lines' are important. Constantly ask questions that will help to bring an understanding of the play. For Act One, Scene One, for example, the following questions might be asked:

(i) When the play opens, what do the plebeians want to do? Why?
(ii) Which are the important lines spoken by the first citizen?

(iii) What is the second citizen trying to do?
(iv) What do the citizen's hope to gain from killing Caius Martius?
(v) What encourages the citizens to move towards the capitol?
(vi) Who prevents them from carrying through their actions?

Now act this out without using the text. If you were a citizen how do you feel about it. Do you support the first citizen or the second citizen? Do you change your mind at all?

In pairs: one be Menenius, the other a citizen; discuss the situation. Menenius to try in his own words to describe the State as that being the body of a man. What do you think Menenius is thinking while he is telling the plebeians this fable?

(vii) Of what is Menenius trying to assure the crowd?
(viii) What is the attitude of Martius towards the crowd?
(ix) What would he do to them if he had his way? Does he mean this?
(x) What is the crowd's reaction to Martius? Why don't they kill him?
(xi) What information does Martius bring?
(xii) How do the crowd receive this news?
(xiii) What is the messenger's news? How does Martius receive this news?
(xiv) How do the crowd receive this news?
(xv) Who is Aufidius and what is the attitude of Martius towards him?
(xvi) What is the attitude of the patricians towards Martius and what is their attitude towards the crowd?
(xvii) What are Tribunes?
(xviii) What is the attitude of Sicinius and Brutus towards Martius?

Once a measure of understanding of what makes these people do what they do, the language will become more easily manageable. As well as acquiring through study the *why* of the people's behaviour, by assuming the roles and behaving in the manner that the text suggests you will most likely discover the *how*. Try to place yourself in the position of the characters.

Notebook

Keep a log book/scrap book while working on *Coriolanus*. Write what you think is the aim of each scene, what you think is the most important piece of information in that scene and what you think is the most important happening. Make a list of the most repeated images in the play (weapons, animals, city). Use pictures to illustrate some of them. Draw some of them. Makes notes on the happenings of the years 1603–9, Sir Walter Raleigh, the London of James I, enclosures. Find pictures of people in city streets, market places, shops, factories, craftsmen, politicians and generals, aristocrats, men fighting with ancient weapons (film stills?), cavalry and armoury, weapons (up to and including 1914–18 war), mothers with one child or baby.

Ideas

Tell the story of *Coriolanus* in four different ways:
(i) Coriolanus as a hero.
(ii) Coriolanus as a villain.
(iii) Tell the story of *Coriolanus* as though it were a secret.
(iv) Tell the story of *Coriolanus* as though telling it to a child.

In pairs: one to be a patrician; the other a plebeian:
(i) As a patrician describe a typical day in your life.
(ii) As a plebeian describe a typical day in your life. Consider shopping, eating, work, home, travel, money, property and your attitude towards these things as either a patrician or a plebeian.
(iii) As a patrician describe a plebeian to other patricians—a plebeian stands there, the centre of the patrician's description.
(iv) As a plebeian, describe a patrician to other plebeians.
(v) Patricians to one side of the acting space and plebeians to the other; in their own way each group is to insult the other.

Hold elections for tribunes. Four, five or six to stand in a 'market place' and give a speech that tells the people of Rome why they should be elected their representatives in the senate. All speeches to be given simultaneously and repeated. Groups of people to move from one speaker to another. They may heckle and finally vote for two representatives.

(i) As a Roman soldier, describe to a fellow soldier how Martius took Corioli.

(ii) As a Volscian widow, describe to a neighbour how the Romans sacked Corioli.
Hold Coriolanus up for trial. He is to be accused of being an enemy of the people. As a witness speak for his defence or prosecution.

As a television commentator describe in contemporary terms, as an eyewitness:
   The plebeians rebelling in the streets
   Martius leading the troops at Corioli
   The triumphal entry into Rome after the victory
   Coriolanus being accused of being a traitor by the tribunes
   The Volscian army advancing on the gates of Rome
   The assassination of Coriolanus
and interview some of the leading characters, and 'men in the street'.

Produce newspapers with drawings and 'political' cartoons as descriptions and comments on the above situations.

Related reading

Coriolanus New Penguin Shakespeare edited by G. R. Hibbard
The Plebeians Rehearse the Uprising Gunter Grass, Secker and Warburg
Shakespeare Our Contemporary Jan Kott, Methuen
Brecht on Theatre edited John Willett, Methuen
Shakespeare in Performance John Russell Brown, Penguin

Related films

The Seven Samurai and *The Magnificent Seven*

b. Contemporary plays

Each generation produces a crop of exciting and meaningful dramatists whose work appeals at the time of their writing. Sometimes this appeal lasts, and the author lives beyond his immediate time. Other plays quickly date and become old-fashioned and meaningless.

In this century the plays of Bernard Shaw, J. B. Priestley, Pirandello, Clifford Odets, Max Frisch, Peter Weiss, John Osborne, Harold Pinter, Arnold Wesker, Brendan Behan, Shelagh Delaney, Eugene O'Neill, Sean O'Casey, Eugene Ionesco, Jean Anouilh, Jean-Paul Sartre, Samuel Beckett, Edward Albee, amongst others are worth constant reference.

The German playwright, Bertolt Brecht, has been particularly influential in this century. Apart from writing some of the most remarkable plays of the time, he has analysed conflicting theatre techniques and evolved a theoretical approach to his work in the theatre. Although his conclusions have not been universally accepted, reflections of his theories are common in plays, films and television programmes. Some of his plays contain a didactic element which disturbs many people—several of them have a direct style which can be seen influencing other plays. His use of traditional aspects of music hall, circuses, fairgrounds, and ideas from film and 'pop' music and radio has led to a style of theatre which is strikingly alert to contemporary issues.

As an example, the influence of his play *Mother Courage* can be seen on an English play of the 50's—John Arden's *Serjeant Musgrave's Dance*.

Mother Courage by Bertolt Brecht
Germany 1938–9

Mother Courage takes place in the Thirty Years' War (1614–48) which spread across the face of Europe. Battles raged continuously. Armies were defeated, recovered and defeated their enemies in turn. The battles were religious—Catholic against Protestant. In the middle of the war, across the path of the battles, trundles an old peasant woman and her children. Mother Courage is a sharp, tough little woman of indeterminate nationality, travelling across the continent selling wares to soldiers. She suffers a succession of defeats, including the death of all her children. She comes to symbolise the courage of humanity against impossible odds. She is a tiny figure in a vast landscape—a landscape of death, destruction, coldness, inhospitality, inhumanity, which she infuses with uncompromising warmth and toughness.

We are not invited to share her grief and ill-fortune. We are invited to watch it. We do not suffer the plight of the soldiers, peasants, priests, cooks and captains; we see them spread out before, as it were on the face of the map of war, with its struggles of power, economics and religion.

Mother Courage tells us about war, but does not act it out. There is no fighting on stage, there are no great battles. All we see is a well-worn canteen wagon getting shabbier as the wars progress, and an old woman getting older. The play shows, in short scenes, moments in the passage of the wagon through Europe, and what happens to Mother Courage. It is a collection of events rather than a continuous one. These events are linked by songs and by messages to the audience, some of which give information as to what is going to happen next. This helps the audience to concentrate upon what is being said, and cuts out the element of suspense and surprise.

Brecht's characters are generally full of vigour. Subtleties of personality are worked in with a series of details. The characters carry the main line of the argument, and since the argument is strong, the actors need to be. The characters are of great humanity and have much opportunity for humour, which is a constant ingredient in the writing of Brecht's characters.

The action, based very firmly in real events and true situations, is transformed into a poetry which is stylised and 'theatricalised'. The designer is all-important. Settings and costumes are related to the social position of the characters and to the materials available to represent the feel of the environment. *Mother Courage* takes place in an environment of destruction and ruin. The characters exist amidst gun-fire and bloodshed, out of doors. They wear clothes that are weathered —they use heavy woollens, leathers and furs. The clothes are worn for a life-time. The wagon is similarly weathered and 'used'. The stage is bare of inessentials. It tells us what we need to know. The wagon. A tent. A house. Nothing unnecessary. We can concentrate on the details. What we do see is finely built and constructed.

'Of course,' Brecht wrote, '... environment had been shown in plays before, not, however, as an independent element but only from the viewpoint of the main figure of the drama. It rose out of the hero's reaction to it ... in the epic theatre it was now to appear as an independent element.

'The stage began to narrate. The narrator no longer vanished with the fourth wall. Not only did the background make its own comment on stage happenings, through large screens which evoked other events occurring at the same time in other places, documenting or contradicting statements by characters through quotations projected onto a screen, lending tangible, concrete statistics to abstract discussions, providing facts and figures for happenings which were plastic but unclear in their meaning; the actors no longer threw themselves completely into their roles but maintained a certain distance from the character performed by them, even distinctly inviting criticism.'

The songs are not stuck on artificially—they are an essential part of the whole. A dissertation by, say, Mother Courage contains seeds which will grow. A speech sometimes grows into a song. They both develop the argument and the theme.

Writing in the middle of a period of brutality and barbarity, it is understandable that Brecht should deal with war, politics, devastation and persecution. Later writers, such as John Arden, were confronted with slightly different happenings; in Arden's case, the bitterness of colonial fighting. *Serjeant Musgrave's Dance* is an original creation, but the influence of style and theatre technique can be traced from Brecht's writings.

Serjeant Musgrave's Dance by John Arden
England 1959

The play

Into a winter landscape, the epitome of all that is nothing, of infertility, of darkness and numbing cold come three soldiers led by their serjeant, Black Jack Musgrave. They carry with them three or four heavy wooden boxes with the broad WD arrow stencilled on them. They are taken by a hunch-backed bargee, along the canal that is rapidly being choked with ice, to a small industrial town somewhere in the North of England. The town is snow-bound, the pit wheels are idle and the colliers are locked-out. The town is starving as the men demand a living wage. The pit owner, who is also the Mayor, has had to cut his wages as the price of coal has fallen. The colliers threatened to strike and the Mayor closed the gates to the pit. The arrival of the soldiers, ostensibly on a recruiting campaign, with drum, colours and the Queen's shilling, add tension to a situation already fraught with pent up violence. The town believes the soldiers to be strike breakers but the pit owners are also able to see them as a welcome diversion and a means to be rid of the trouble-makers. The soldiers, however, are in this particular town for their own purposes. They are neither strike breakers nor on a recruiting campaign but have deserted and come to preach at gun point, the gospel of peace.

The themes of the play are imbued with violence; and the violence is contagious. The soldiers fight among themselves, one of the band is killed by the others and led by their serjeant, who despite the tragedy, is determined to carry through his terrible plan. In the Market Square, under banners and flags and the Victorian clock-tower-cum-lamp-post-cum-market cross, and with patriotic slogans echoing in their ears, the contents of the boxes are revealed: rifles and ammunition, a loaded gatling gun that swivels and holds the panicking townspeople in their place and a skeleton in uniform is hoisted upon an arm of the cross. The serjeant explains the purpose of his mission. The skeleton is that of Billy Hicks, who once lived in that town. He had been shot in the back by local patriots while overseas where his regiment was stationed to guard a

Serjeant Musgrave's Dance. The pugnacious collier and Sparky.

British Protectorate. Under orders British soldiers entered the city searching for the killers and caused the death of five people of that city. And in the inexorable logic of military arithmetic Musgrave has decided that this five must again be multiplied by five. Twenty-five of the people present in the Market Place must be killed.

The characters

Serjeant Musgrave is a religious fanatic, whose pseudo-evangelical theories serve only to mask a blind urge to destroy. Arden describes him as 'tall, commanding, sardonic, but never humorous; he could well have served under Cromwell'. He is a cold man and hard: 'The North Wind in a pair of millstones/Was your father and your mother . . .' A regular soldier, a professional who 'works his life to bugle and drum . . . You ever see him late?' His orders are sharp and he expects to be obeyed. However, he sleeps uneasily and sees in a nightmare fire, burning, destruction, and the end of the world. The effect of war and killing plagues his conscience, and unhinges his sense of balance so that he believes himself to be God's avenging angel. He feels he has the divine right, that God was with him, to call a parade and to end violence with violence. In the final scene he is still 'blind'. His logic was without love therefore he was destined to fail.

Sparky, the youngest of the soldiers, realises that someone was responsible for his comrades death, but he is confused and dies, accidentally stabbed by a bayonet in a scuffle, trying to escape from what he doesn't understand.

Hurst, the wild killer, the animal of the four, lives for his 'eye for an eye' dream. 'Bloody minded, quick-tempered, cynical, tough . . .', the murderer of the four.

Attercliffe, the oldest, is awakening from a life of soldiering to realise that he, like Sparky, was confused. However, in the last scene he acquires some perception and tells Musgrave that it was no bloody good trying to end war by its own rules. 'Sparky died of those damned rules.'

The Mayor, the Parson, and the Constable each represent their areas of the 'Establishment': the employer/local politician, the church and the law. They are primarily responsible for the violence, and they condone it by their refusal to face up to it. They hide behind a wall of stock responses.

The Bargee acts occasionally as the chorus; he changes factions to his own advantage. He is the crooked man, similar in some respects to Chaplin who cocks a snook at authority 'and has a natural urge towards intrigue and mischief'. He is the clown who opts in and out of the action, comments on it and occasionally winds it up and sets it in motion. It is he who starts the singing of 'Michael Finnegan', it is he who brings the soldiers into the town

The colliers 'are all embittered' and prepared to fight for their existence with 'fists and pick hefts and stones and feet. If you work in the coal seam you carry iron on your clogs—see!' Their appearance may be described '. . . as strange and slightly sinister. Their exhausted faces, with the grime clinging to the hollows, have a fierce, wild look . . . They have a very upright square-shouldered walk, reaction from the constant bending underground, but most are shortish men and their thick ill-fitting clothes hide the splendour of their bodies.' George Orwell, *The Road to Wigan Pier*.

Mrs. Hitchcock, the landlady, who sits in her bar room and watches and listens to everything that happens is 'a woman of deep sympathies and intelligence, which she disguises by north country sombre pessimism'. She sees things for what they are: 'This strike is bad for the town . . . that means me . . . means you too. And it means His Worship the Mayor . . .' It is she who tells Musgrave that he tried his lesson the wrong way that although he wished to end war, he had brought a different war; he had brought anarchy.

Annie, the tavern whore, the big-boned, aggressive girl who provoked the men. Although she may be emotionally confused it is she who has the clarity of vision. She knows life and death: Billy Hicks had been her lover and she had had his baby who had died in childbirth, a mutant '. . . a twisted little dead thing that nobody laughed at.' It is she who knows 'for what a soldier is good,' and it is she who exposes the sham of Musgrave's philosophy and following, and the pettiness of her fellow townspeople for being taken in. 'Take a sight of this you hearty colliers; see what they've brought you.' But they don't see, neither does Musgrave, although she holds up the dead soldier's jacket pierced by a bayonet and stained in blood standing beneath the rotting skeleton of her murdered lover: the soldiers have brought further violence and bloodshed.

The setting

John Arden in his introduction asks for no scenery or props, except what is necessary for the action and those pieces to be absolutely authentic, 'so that the audience see a selection from the details of everyday life rather than a generalised impression: a drum, weapons, the boxes, etc. He further suggests that the paintings of L. S. Lowry might suggest a suitable mood.

Like this, the town of the play is the 'coldest town I ever was in' with 'empty streets, locked doors, windows blind, shops cold and empty . . . no chimneys smoking, no horses . . .' The colours are 'red uniforms, in a black and white coalfield'. The black is for the coalmine and for death, the red is for soldiers 'the blood red roses' and for murder. The colliers wish to change their black for the soldier's red. The landscape is white from which pitheads stand like stark metal skeletons which, in turn suggest a metal cage inside of which all are trapped, snowbound, and cut off from the rest of the world. Although there is a clear indication of place, the exact date of the action is deliberately not given. Because of the action and the language it suggests the nineteenth century rather than the twentieth. The scarlet uniforms, the Queen's shilling, the recruiting of soldiers under the influence of beer suggest a less sophisticated method than one employed now.

The language

Serjeant Musgrave's Dance has much in common with the traditional ballad in that it concerns itself with vivid action and with a sense of the sensational and melodramatic. John Arden has also found a style of language that is close in texture to that of the ballad and has written his play with a mixture of verse, prose and song. His songs will fit the melodies of traditional English folk songs, while the verse may be heightened by either accompanying them with a drum rhythm or by composing original music which is in sympathy with the style of the play. Naturally, much of the language is an amalgam of North country dialects. It is hard, highly coloured and occasionally very powerful, matching the action.

The Empire wars are far away
For duty's sake we sail away
My arms and legs is shot away
And all for the wink of a shilling and a drink . . .

I'll tell you for what a soldier's good:
To march behind his roaring drum,
Shout to us all: 'Here I come
I've killed as many as I could—
I'm stamping into your fat town
From the war and to the war
And every girl can be my whore
Just watch me lay them squealing down
And that's what he does and so do we
Because we know he'll soon be dead
We strap our arms around the scarlet red
Then send him weeping over the sea.

I'm doing here? I'm doing . . . Serjeant, you know it. 'Cos he died. That wor Billy. I got drunk. Four days and four nights. After work of one night. Absent. Not sober. Improperly dressed.

Stick me in a cell boys
Pull the prison bell
Black Jack Musgrave
To call the prison roll.

Sarn't no offence—'First ye'll serve your punishment,' he says. 'Then I'll show you how,' he says, the Serjeant. I says, 'You show me what?' He says, 'I'll show you how your Billy can be paid for' . . . I didn't want to pay for him what did I care for a colonial war? . . . But I did want to pay for him didn't I? 'Cos that's why I'm here . . .

Black Jack Musgrave
He always calls the roll.

He says:
Go down to Billy's town
Tell 'em how he died.

And that's what I'm doing here. The serjeant pays the fare. Here I am, I'm paid for. Next turn's for Billy. Or all that's left of Billy. Who'll give me an offer for his bones? Sixpence for a bone, for a bone of my dead mucker . . .

We are here with a word. That's all. That's particular. Let the word dance. That's all that's material, this day and for the next. What happens afterwards the Lord God will provide. I am with you, he said. Abide with Me in Power. A Pillar of Flame before the people. What we show here will lead forward forever, against dishonour, and greed, and murder-for-greed! There is our duty, the new deserters duty: God's dance on this earth: and all that we are is His four strong legs to dance it.

Chorus: Blow your morning bugles boys
　　　　Blow your calls ey-ho
　　　　Form platoons and dress the ranks
　　　　and blow boys blow

Fire, fire! fire, fire, London's burning, London's burning! Burning, burning One minute from now, and you carry out your orders—get *that* one! *Get* her! Who says she's a child! We've got her in the book, she's old enough to kill! You will carry out your orders. Thirty seconds. Count the time. Twenty-six . . . twenty-three . . . Twenty . . . Eighteen . . . I'm on duty . . . I'm timing the end of the world. Ten more seconds, sir . . . Five . . . three . . . two . . . *one*.

For the apple holds a seed will grow
In live and lengthy joy
To raise a flourishing tree of fruit
For ever and a day.
With fal-la-la-the-dee-toor-a-ley,
For ever and a day.

They're going to hang us up a length higher nor most apple trees grow, Serjeant. D'you reckon we can start an orchard?

Improvisation as an introduction to the play

In groups of five or six set up the stealing of the money from the regimental company's offices.

Imagine how four deserters would get aboard a ship to bring them home to England?
　　Would they have bought their passage home?
　　What about their unusual baggage?
　　Would they have stowed aboard?
　　How would they have coped with officials on
　　　　the boat?
　　Would they have worked their passage home?
　　How would they have coped with questions
　　　　about who they are and what they are doing?

Possible conversations between the townspeople
　　An interview between the Mayor and Walsh
　　over the reasons for the cut in wages.
　　A collier and his wife when he tells her that the
　　mine owners have decided to cut their wages.

Groups of townspeople tell of likely stories about the Mayor
　　the Parson
　　the Constable
　　the Bargee
　　Annie
　　the arrival of the soldiers and why they
　　are there.

Read the scenes in the play and improvise them.
　　The soldiers playing cards waiting for Musgrave in the numbing cold.
　　The arrival at the ale house and the reception by Mrs. Hitchcock.
　　The soldiers meeting the out-of-work colliers in the graveyard.
　　The ale house where the colliers meet the soldiers and over ale sing and dance; the climax being the arrival of the Constable.
　　The crazy drill; the colliers using pick hefts as rifles and being drilled by the Bargee.
　　In the stables and the teasing of Sparky which ends in his death.

Offshoots

Like *The Government Inspector* the play involves the incursion of strangers into a small community. This story may also be aligned in similarity with that of a Western film. Here the community are living at the level of survival and are under the influence of the town's officers. Imagine a small Western town, possibly in desert country where the town has the only source of water for many miles until the rains come. Into this community come deserters from the Unionist Army at the time of the civil war. They are there to seek revenge, for at some time a member of that town betrayed or killed a relation of one of the deserters. And like *Musgrave* the apparently inevitable bloodshed is avoided by the arrival of the Cavalry.

Related reading

The Road to Wigan Pier George Orwell, Penguin
The Ballad Book edited by M. Leach, Thomas Yossolop

Other plays by John Arden include:
Live Like Pigs
Ars Longa Vita Brevis
The Business of Good Government
The Royal Pardon

The Family of Man

The Family of Man

Some years ago the Metropolitan Museum of Modern Art in New York mounted an exhibition of photographs which toured the world. It was called *The Family of Man* and was a collection of some of the most important photographs taken of people from different nations engaged in aspects of living. It showed such things as celebrations, work, families and children and revealed a similarity between the way different peoples live—contrasting habits and customs.

The section that follows uses the idea of this exhibition (later published as a book) as a starting point—how people live and have lived. Using some of the techniques previously discussed (including slides, music, movement, lights, film, dance, song) a collage is built up exploring aspects of life. The material itself is totally flexible, indeed dispensible—other pieces can be added, the outline changed, the approach redefined.

If a copy of the book, *The Family of Man*, can be found, use it as a source for ideas, together with the material given here, and then evolve a collage which aims to suggest that man, in spite of wars, illness and destruction, has within him the power and ability to survive.

Preliminary activities

Discuss the various stages through which people pass during their lifetime, and the different things that could happen during these stages. Make a series of headings, such as 'Birth', 'Childhood', 'Adolescence', 'Marriage', 'Death', etc. and under each heading start to list any sources of ideas that can be used for drama. Stories about people you know, books that you have read, songs that you know and like, and such items can be added to the list. When the list seems to be complete, select some of the items on the list and use these as the basis for improvisation. Other things on the list, such as a song or a poem, may suggest other forms of treatment—a group chant, or a solo song.

Divide into groups and begin to work on ideas that appeal to each group, perhaps taking different items from the list. Each group should begin to add ideas of their own, and make a collection of photographs and drawings of things which relate to the project. Each group should start to look at libraries and magazines and collections of stories and poems, and find items that excite and interest them, to do with the way people live and have lived in different parts of the world and at different times.

When each group has made a collection of a few items, the whole group can begin to assemble the material they have been working on. Gaps will be found, and some items will either seem to be repetitive or too long. The next stage is to organise all the material into a shape. Some of the items will appear out of place. These should be cut. Other headings will seem to be scantily treated, more information should be found. Eventually, the collection of items will make a balanced whole which flows from item to item. To give the whole coherence, the group needs to be organised as one group, rather than a series of separate ones, working together to show *The Family of Man*.

Finally, the whole needs to be seen in terms of presentation. All the ideas and methods suggested in various parts of these books can be used, and any others that have come to light during the work done in drama over a period of time. Such a presentation can make use of all the talents of the group, from the technically-minded to the musician, in just as much time and space as each person feels able to contribute.

Darkness.
A dull sound. Thudding.
Distant wind. Thudding. Growling. Groaning. The
sounds move through the darkness. They shuffle,
rush, speed by. They grow in volume. They fill the
space. They come and they go.
A breathing. A primitive whimpering.

Light.
A dull light. Throbbing.
A distant glow. Throbbing. Changing. Swirling.
The lights slowly throb around and through the
space. There are mists. Shapes. Irregular. Still.
Gaunt. The lights throb and glow. Red. Green.
Purple. Brown. The dim shapes can be seen through
the colours. A pin-point is left. Fading into the
distance.

Music.
A primitive reed-like sound. Drums.

Words.
Grunts with recognisable 'open' sounds. The begin-
nings of words.

Light.
Rising, throbbing. Colours changing.

Sounds.
Music, words, breathing, groaning—all rising.

Movement.
The shapes of figures scramble and roll, grapple and
turn, rising and falling, closing and opening.

Sound, light, movement, combine to a rising unity.
   They stop.
   A dull, dim, picture is held of shapes in confusion.
   Of clouds and mists.

Voice *speaks*:
In the beginning God created the heaven and the earth.
And the earth was without form and void and the darkness was upon the face of the deep.
And the spirit of God moved upon the face of the waters.
And God said, Let there be light, and there was light.
And God called the Light Day, and the Darkness he called Night.
And the evening and the morning were the first day.

The shapes organise themselves into a mass. When it is still for a moment it divides into two groups, which are still. Light comes up on the figures.

Voice:

At the dawn of time there was neither sand nor icy waves. The earth did not exist. Nor the sky. Nowhere did grass grow. Only a yawning abyss stretched through space. A land of clouds and shadows, formed in the regions to the north from which spread the glacial waters of twelve rivers. To the south lay the land of fire. From there poured rivers whose waters contained a bitter poison which little by little set and became solid. On contact with the ice from the north this first deposit became covered with thick coatings of hoar frost which partly filled the abyss. But the warm air blowing from the south began to melt the ice; and from the tepid drops which thus formed was born a giant in human form—the first of all living beings.

Teutonic myth

A loud crunching noise. A dropping sound. The figures one by one fall away from their mass, and together form a shape, that of a sleeping giant. The figures make up the body, the arms, the legs, and the head. A white light comes over the area, spreading slowly, but growing in intensity.

Voice:

Thus there is a white god, god of light and day, and a black god, god of the shadows and of night: a god of good and a god of evil, thus a dualism: the opposition between light and the creative force, and darkness and the destructive force.

Slavonic myth

Drums. Thunder. Darkness. The shape of the giant is seen to stir. Limbs struggle. The head moves. Parts of the body writhe. Figures struggle within its shape. Screams. Fights.

The shape starts to break up. Figures rise and confront each other.

A heavy, slow, loud and deadly battle breaks out, with thunder, screams and menacing sounds.

A loud metallic crash booms through the battle. The figures look up. Looming through them is a giant figure who lumbers through the confusion. He scatters the figures. He is huge, with fearsome, impressive features.

He stands. The figures are still.

Michelangelo's 'Creation'.

Voice:

After the great battle Marduk organised the world. He built a dwelling place for the gods in the sky and installed the stars in their image; he fixed the length of the year and regulated the course of the heavenly bodies. Thus the earth was formed and Marduk created humanity moulding from blood the body of the first man. *Assro-Babylonian Myth*

The figures move into a circle. In the centre, lying on the ground under a huge sheet, is another figure. The giant goes to it, and the figure, clad in the giant sheet, rises. The giant turns. On his back is moulded another set of features, another giant equally fearsome and awe-inspiring.

Voice:

Juok was the god who created all men on earth. In the land of the Whites he found white earth or sand, and made it into men of the same colour. Then he came to Egypt where he made brown men from the Nile mud and then to Shilluk and created the Black from the black earth. Then Juok said: 'I shall make man but he must run and walk, so I will give him two long legs like those of the flamingoes'. That done, he said, 'Man must be able to cultivate millet, so I shall give him two arms—one to use the hoe, and the other to pull up weeds'. Then he said: 'I shall give man two eyes to see with'. And so he did. Then he said: 'I shall give him a mouth to eat his millet.' And then he gave him a tongue and ears so that he could shout, dance, sing, speak and listen to noises and speeches.

Thus man was made perfect.

Myth from the Shilluk people of the White Nile

During this speech, the sheet is taken off the figure, and the god gives the man the eyes, arms and legs, ears and mouth that he mentions. The man slowly becomes aware of himself. Feeling spreads through him. The figures surround him, as he slowly feels the sensations of living. He says, softly at first :

I am a man.

And repeats this more loudly. Finally he says :

I am a man. I can

shout *he does this*	listen *he does this*
dance *he does this*	sing *he does this*
	speak *he is doing this*

As he is listening, another of the figures turns, becomes aware of himself and says :

I am a man. I can shout etc.

One after another the figures join in, until the whole group is singing, dancing, etc.

A loud gong fills the area. They all turn and face the giant Juok.

Voice:

Man must cultivate millet.

Voice:

And the Lord God took the man, and put him in the Garden of Eden to dress it and keep it.

Juok goes.

The people take up hoes, and scythes and spades and forks, and they dig the land, and tend the trees. They plant and reap and tend the crops. Rain beats down. They work on. Then comes intense heat, burning down. They continue with their work. Finally cold winter comes. The ground is hard, the air is cold. The people put away their implements, and huddle together. A cold wind. A cold light. No movement.

Voice:

And the Lord God caused a deep sleep to fall upon Adam and he slept: and he took one of his ribs, and closed up the flesh instead thereof: And the rib, which the Lord God had taken from man, made he a woman, and brought her unto the man (Genesis 2).

The slumbering figures stir. The women figures rise, cautiously and gently look around them, and find their way to a sleeping man. They stay with the man. The wind rises. The light grows brighter.

Voice:

The first woman was named Pandora. She was made in heaven, every god contributing something to perfect her. She was conveyed to Earth and presented to Epimetheus, the God who himself had made man. In his home he had a jar containing certain unpleasant items which he had excluded when he had made man. Pandora was seized with an eager curiosity to know what this jar contained; and one day she slipped off the cover and looked in. Forthwith there escaped a multitude of plagues for hapless man, such as gout, rheumatism and colic for his body, and envy, spite and revenge for his mind. The whole contents of the jar escaped, except for hope. So we see to this day, whatever evils are abroad, hope never entirely leaves us. *A Greek myth*

The figures stir in pain and agony, illness and fever.
They struggle and try to rise. Rain forces them
down. Slowly, the sun rises. Winter falls away.
Spring rises. They feel warmer, happier. They cast
off the drudgery of winter and of illness. They start
to revive, and move. They start to sing and dance.
A Spring Dance.

Voice:

To every thing there is a season, and a time to
every purpose under the heaven.

A time to be born, and a time to die; a time to
plant, and a time to pluck up that which is
planted;

A time to kill, and a time to heal; a time to break
down, and a time to build up;

A time to weep, and a time to laugh; a time to
mourn, and a time to dance;

A time to cast away stones, and a time to gather
stones together;

A time to embrace, and a time to refrain from
embracing;

A time to get, and a time to lose; a time to keep,
and a time to cast away;

A time to rend, and a time to sew; a time to keep
silence, and a time to speak;

A time to love, and a time to hate; a time of war,
and a time of peace.   *Ecclesiates 3*

A large white screen descends
Words are picked out on the screen

SEASONS BIRTH DEATH SOW REAP KILL HEAL
DESTROY BUILD CRY LAUGH MOURN DANCE
THROW AWAY COLLECT EMBRACE WIN LOSE
KEEP TEAR SEW SILENCE SPEAKING LOVE HATE
WAR PEACE . . .

A quiet song fills the area. A flute plays a melody.

Voice:

The voice of my beloved! behold, he cometh leaping upon the mountains skipping upon the hills.

My beloved is like a roe or a young hart: behold, he standeth behind our wall,

He looketh forth at the windows, shewing himself through the lattice.

My beloved spake and said unto me, 'Rise up, my love, my fair one, and come away.

For lo, the winter is past, and the rain is over and gone;

The flowers appear on the earth; the time of the singing of birds is come, and the voice of the turtle
   is heard in our land;

The fig tree putteth forth her green figs, and the vines with the tender grapes give a good smell.
   Arise my love, my fair one, and come away.

O my dove, that art in the clefts of the rock, in the secret places of the stairs, let me see thy
   countenance, let me hear thy voice, and thy countenance is comely.

Take us the foxes, the little foxes, that spoil our vines; for our vines have tender grapes.

My beloved is mine, and I am his; he feedeth among the lilies.

Until the day break, and the shadows flee away, turn, my beloved, and be though like a roe or a
   young hart among the mountains of Bether.   From *The Song of Solomon*

The flute continues playing.
Angelic voices sing : Gloria in Excelsis.
An angel appears. The light grows bright. The
music swells.
The angel goes, the arena is cleared.
Enter three shepherds.

3rd   Brother, look up and behold:
shepherd: What thing is yonder that shineth so bright?
1st   As long as ever I have watched my fold,
shepherd: Yet saw I never such a sight
     In field or in lea.
3rd: Hark they sing above in the clouds so clear:
     Heard I never so merry a choir.
1st: Fellows in fear,
     May you not hear?
     'Tis music on high.
2nd: Aye, of glore and of 'glere'. . . .
3rd: Now, gentle brothers, draw we near
     To hear their harmony.
1st: Yet no man is near
     That I can espy.

The angel Gabriel sings

Gabriel *singing*: Hark, herdsmen, awake! Of loving I call!
     He is born for your sake, Lord Perpetual.
     He is come for to take and ransom you all
     From taint and from teen.
          A child is born
    At Bethlem this morn.
    You shall find him ere dawn
    Two beasts between.

Music rises and fades in the distance

1st: Ah God, ah, dear dominus, what was this song?
3rd: He spoke of a bairn,
     We must seek him, I you warn,
     That betokens yon star,
     That stands yonder out.
1st: That same is he that *prophets* foretold! . . .
     That in the winter's night so cold,
     God's son, should be born in a child's mould
     Of a maiden that should him hold.
     Yet still I doubt what it meaneth to us—

Brueghel: Booth drama at a village fete.

Gabriel *singing*: Ye lowly herdsmen,
          Dread ye nothing
          Of this star that ye do see.
          For this same morn
              God's son is born
          In Bethlem of a maiden free.
          Hie you hither in haste:
          Ye shall find him 'ere dawn
          Two beasts between.

2nd: 'Twas a wondrous tune, it can scarce be denied. . . .

3rd: Come, forth let us run; we may not abide!

2nd: No light maketh the moon, 'tis dark at this tide.

1st: Nay Dick have done; the star will us guide.
          Bethlem is not far
      Let us do his hest.

3rd: That hold I best.

1st: Then must we go east
      And follow the star
      Where the star doth glow
      Make we our way.

3rd: Aye, eye, hie we quickly;

1st: Now wend we forth to Bethlehem;

All *singing*: 'As I rode out this ender's night
      Of three jolly shepherds I saw a sight;
      They sang terli, terli, terlow,
      So merrily the shepherds their pipes gan blow;
      Of three jolly shepherds I saw a sight,
      All about their fold a star shone bright;
      They sang terli, terli, terlow,
      So merrily the shepherds their pipes 'gan blow . . .'

1st: The place is now near; art thou ready and yare?

3rd: That he would appear to so poor as we are
      In sooth makes me fear. . . .

1st: Nay, follow the star:
      Look lo, to yon light!
      Abide, sirs, a space: yonder, lo!
      That stable is the place; come on let us go.
      'Tis so by my beard.

2nd: Thou must go in first.

1st: Nay, thinkst thou I durst?

3rd: Nay be not afeared. . . .
      But knock on the door, herdsmen, knock: for I swear
      No woe, but God's bliss thereby shall you win.

1st: I prithee, go first.

3rd: Nay, I be too young of age.

2nd: And I be too curst.

1st: Nay then—and *I* will. . . .
      Hail, maid-mother and wife so mild,
      To thee and thy son I kneel to the ground.
      I have nothing to present to thy child,
      But my pipe.

Blows a few notes

	Hold, hold, take it in thy hand,
	Where in much pleasure have I ever found.
	And now to honour thy glorious birth,
	Thou shalt it take to make the mirth.
2nd:	Now hail be thou, child, and thy dame.
	Though in a poor manger here art thou laid.
	So the angel said and told us thy name.
	Hold, take thou my hat on thy head.
3rd:	Hail be thou, Lord, over waters and lands!
	For thy coming all we may make mirth. . . .
1st & 2nd:	Aye, aye.
3rd:	Have here my mittens to put on thy hands
1st:	Lo, merry he is!
	Lo, he laughs; my sweeting;
	A welcome meeting!
	I have given my greeting:—
	Have a bob of cherries.

all laugh

2nd:	A bird have I brought
	To my bairn from afar,
	See the bird goeth hop,
	Thou little day-star.
3rd:	My heart would bleed
	To see thee sit here in so poor a weed,
	With no pennies.
	Before thee I fall
	And give thee this ball
	Have and play thee withal,
	And go to the tennis. . . .
1st:	Sooth, now I have no more to say;
	Farewell, mine own dear darling.
2nd:	Fair child, now have good day.
3rd:	Farewell, my lord and my sweeting.
1st *going:*	Farewell, born in poor array.
2nd *going:*	Farewell.
3rd *going:*	Till our next meeting.
2nd:	Now go we forth bold.
1st:	'Twas a wonder to see; now a fig for the cold!
3rd:	Forsooth, e'en already it seems to betold
	Full oft.
1st:	What grace have we found.
	Well, let's forth to our ground.
	To sing are we bound
	And to praise him aloft!
All *singing:*	'A-down from heaven, from heaven so high,
	Of angels there came a company,
	They sang terli, terlow, terli,
	With mirth and great solemnity.
	Terli, terlow, terli, terlow!
	So merrily the shepherds their pipes 'gan blow. . . .'

Singing fades into the distance   From *The Wakefield Cycle* Medieval Mystery Play

Adventure playground.

Screen: *Picture of new-born baby, still connected with umbilical cord.*

Song:

I sing of a maiden
That is makeless, (matchless)
King of all kings
To her son she ches.
He came al so stille
There his moder was
As dew in Aprille
That falleth on the grass.
He came all so stille,
To his moder's hour,
As dew in Aprille
That falleth on the flour.
He came al so stille
There his moder lay.
As dew in Aprille
That falleth on the spray.
Moder and mayden
Was never none but she:
Well may such a lady
Goddes moder be.

Medieval Carol

Voice Announces:

BIRTHS. *Anderson*—on 19th May 1970 to Diane and George Anderson—a daughter (Harriet)

Aslockton—on 20th May 1970 at 35 Smith's Terrace, SW1, to Pamela and Leonard Aslockton, a second son (Christopher Robert).

Voice:

Dear Vernon,

This is just to tell you that Caitlin and I have a son aged 48 hours. Its name is Llewelyn Thomas. It is red-faced, very angry and blue-eyed. Bit blue, bit green. It does not like the world. Caitlin is well and beautiful.   *Letter from Dylan Thomas*

The group become like a group of children. They erupt into a game of 'tag'. They then divide up and start to play a whole series of children's games in small groups, games such as leap-frog, hop-scotch, piggy-in-the-middle, skipping games.

Screen: *Pictures of children playing.*

103

Ladders, boxes, barrels, planks = play.

Voices:

A tutor who tooted the flute
Tried to tutor two tooters to toot
Said the two to the tutor
Is it harder to toot, or
To tutor two tooters to toot?

Voices:

There's no need to light a night-light
On a night like tonight
For a night-light's a slight light
On a night like tonight

Voices:

A woman to her son did utter
Go, my son, and shut the shutter
The shutter's shut, the son did utter.
I cannot shut it any shutter.

Voices:

How much wood could a woodchuck chuck
If a woodchuck could chuck wood?
A woodchuck would chuck
All the wood he could chuck
If a woodchuck could chuck wood

Each of the verses is spoken by a small group very quickly, but so that the words can be understood. Then the whole group of voices start together and get quicker and quicker. Those playing games speed up the tempo of their playing until the whole group give up exhausted.

Screen: *Drawings and paintings by children.*

The group form a circle with one person in the middle. (The prisoner)

Prisoner: Open wide the garden gate
The garden gate, the garden gate
Open wide the garden gate
And let me through.

The others hold hands. They say:

Get the key to the garden gate
The garden gate, the garden gate
Get the key to the garden gate
And let yourself through.

Prisoner: I've lost the key to the garden gate,
So what am I to do?

Others *circling menacingly:*

Then you may stop, may stop all night,
Within the gate,
Until you're strong enough, you know,
To break a way through.

The prisoner tries to break through the circle. When he does, the circle breaks, and the others run. The prisoner captures one of them, and the caught one goes in the middle. He (or she) stands for a second. The others form a circle around him. Then the circle breaks, and the group splits into twos, one girl and one boy in each pair. The girl who was in the middle sings to her partner:

I don't want to play in your yard
I don't like you any more
You'll be sorry when you see me
Sliding down our cellar door
You can't holler down our rain-barrel
You can't climb our cherry tree
And I don't want to play in your yard
If you won't be good to me.

The boys and girls move around in couples, stand holding hands.

Screen: *Pictures of teenagers.*

Screen: *A series of pictures from a girl's romance story.*

A girl appears as Faith Curtis. A boy appears as Mick, the Ladykiller. As each picture appears they assume the position of the character in the picture, repeating the words in the bubbles. They then develop the plot until they arrive at the situation in the next picture. They then freeze, assume the positions of the next pictures, repeat the words and continue. Other characters can be introduced. Pop-music and coloured lights could accompany the idea.

Well, here goes. And please don't let me make a mess of it!

A date to remember
a date Mick would never forget!

BOY, HOW MY PALS WOULD HAVE LAUGHED TO SEE ME...MICK, THE LADYKILLER, TREMBLING OVER A DATE WITH A GIRL!

IF ONLY THEY KNEW! I'M THE ORIGINAL SHEEP IN WOLF'S CLOTHING.

WHO KNOWS HOW I PLUCKED UP COURAGE TO DATE A SMART JUDY LIKE FAITH CURTIS?

DON'T DO ME ANY FAVOURS. JUST THOUGHT YOU MIGHT LIKE A CHANGE FROM ALL THOSE DROOPS THEY SAY YOU GO OUT WITH.

DOING ANYTHING SATURDAY, SWEETHEART? MIGHT SHOW YOU A GOOD TIME.

ME GO OUT WITH YOU? BUT I HAVE PLENTY OF DATES ALREADY!

WHY NOT? YOU COULDN'T BE ANY WORSE THAN ANY OTHER BOY. ALL RIGHT, I'LL COME.

SO HERE WE WERE...ME TRYING TO STOP MY KNEES TREMBLING, AND SHE LOOKING GREAT.

RELAX, HONEY, HERE'S YOUR HANDSOME MAN. HOPE YOU DIDN'T MIND WAITING.

THAT ALL DEPENDS. WHAT'S ON THE MENU?

THOUGHT WE'D SEE THE POP SHOW AT THE GRANADA.. THEY'RE HOLDING TWO TICKETS FOR ME. MAYBE HAVE A BITE TO EAT FIRST...

COULD BE WORSE. SHALL WE GO?

THAT'S WHEN THINGS STARTED TO GO WRONG.

HEY, TAXI! WHY WON'T THE THINGS STOP FOR ME?

WOULDN'T IT BE QUICKER TO GET A BUS?

THE END

Voice:

Oh but Wendy, when the carpet yielded to my indoor pumps
    There you stood, your gold hair streaming, handsome in the hall-light gleaming
There you looked and there you led me off into the game of clumps
    Then the new Victrola playing
    And your funny uncle saying
'Choose your partners for a fox-trot!
Dance until its *tea* o'clock!
    Come on young'uns, foot it featly!'
    Was it chance that paired us neatly,
        I, who loved you so completely,
You, who pressed me close to you, hard against your party frock?

'Meet me when you've finished eating!' So we met and no one found us.
    Oh that dark and furry cupboard while the rest played hide and seek!
Holding hands our two hearts beating in the bedroom silence round us,
    Holding hands and hardly hearing sudden footstep, thud and shriek.
Love that lay too deep for kissing—
'Where *is* Wendy? Wendy's missing!'
    Love so pure it *had* to end,
Love so strong that I was frighten'd
When you gripped my fingers tight and
    Hugging, whispered 'I'm your friend'.

John Betjeman from Indoor Games Near Newbury

*A few bars of a 1920's tinny record. Then a current
pop-song. The group break out into a dance.*

Screen: *Pictures of current idols, singers, film-
stars, football stars. Also pictures of young people
engaged in various activities, some of them serious
(helping old people, engaged in protests, making
speeches).*

Voice:

Spread thy close curtain, love-performing night,
That runaway's eyes may wink, and Romeo
Leap to these arms untalkt-of and unseen.
Lovers can see to do their amorous rites
By their own beauties; or, if love be blind,
It best agrees, with night.—Come, civil night,
Thou sober-suited matron, all in black,
And learn me how to lose a winning match,
Play'd for a pair of stainless maidenhoods:
Hood my unmann'd blood, bating in my cheeks,   Come, gentle night,—come loving, black-brow'd
With thy black mantle: till strange love, grown   night,
                                    bold,   Give me my Romeo; and, when he shall die,
Think true love acted simple modesty.   Take him and cut him out in little stars,
Come, night; come, Romeo; come, thou day in   And he will make the face of heaven so fine,
                                    night;   That all the world will be in love with night,
For thou wilt lie upon the wings of night   And pay no worship to the garish sun.
Whiter than new snow on a raven's back.—   Romeo and Juliet

108

Song:

Are you going to Scarborough Fair?
Parsley, Sage, Rosemary and Thyme.
Remember me to one who lived there,
For once she was a true love of mine.

Tell her to make me a cambric shirt—
Parsley, Sage, Rosemary and Thyme—
Without any seam or needlework.
She shall be a true love of mine.

Tell her to wash it in yonder dry well—
Parsley, Sage, Rosemary and Thyme—
Where water ne'er sprung nor drop of rain fell.
She shall be a true love of mine.

Tell her to dry it on yonder thorn—
Parsley, Sage, Rosemary and Thyme—
Where blossom ne'er grew since Adam was born.
She shall be a true love of mine.

Well, will you find me an acre of land—
Parsley, Sage, Rosemary and Thyme—
Between the sea foam and the sea sand?
You shall be a true love of mine.

And will you plough it with a lamb's horn—
Parsley, Sage, Rosemary and Thyme—
And sow it all over with one peppercorn?
And you shall be a true love of mine.

Will you reap it with a sickle of leather—
Parsley, Sage, Rosemary and Thyme—
And tie it all up with a peacock's feather?
And you shall be a true love of mine.

And when you've done and you've finished
your work—
Parsley, Sage, Rosemary and Thyme—
Then come to me for your cambric shirt,
And you shall be a true love of mine.

Traditional. *Scarborough Fair*

The couples come together and stand.

Screen: *A young man and young woman together.*

Voice:
He was already stepping on to the threshold, and closing the door behind him. She turned into the kitchen, startled out of herself by this invasion from the night. He took off his hat and came towards her. Then he stood in the light, in his black clothes and his black stock, hat in one hand and yellow flowers in the other. She stood away, at his mercy, snatched out of herself. She did not know him, only she knew he was a man come for her. She could only see the dark-clad man's figure standing there upon her, and the gripped fist of flowers. She could not see the face and the living eyes.

He was watching her, without knowing her, only aware underneath of her presence.

'I come to have a word with you,' he said, striding forward to the table, laying down his hat and the flowers, which tumbled apart and lay in a loose heap. She had flinched from his advance. She had no will, no being. The wind boomed in the chimney, and he waited. He had disembarrassed his hands. Now he shut his fists.

He was aware of her standing there unknown, dread, yet related to him.

'I came up,' he said, speaking curiously matter-of-fact and level, 'to ask if you'd marry me. You are free, aren't you?'

There was a long silence, whilst his blue eyes, strangely impersonal, looked into her eyes to seek an answer to the truth. He was looking for the truth out of her. And she, as if hypnotised, must answer at length.

'Yes, I am free to marry.'

D. H. Lawrence. *The Rainbow*

The Wedding March booms out.

Screen: *Photograph of a young couple getting married.*

Screen: *A series of illustrations from magazines and newspapers of wedding dresses, rings, washing machines, home goods, and other items presumed attractive to newly-weds.*
A 'bride' and a 'groom' stand in the centre. 'Guests' appear with gifts which they place before the couple. The group then break out into celebration. They dance a wedding dance.

Screen: Brueghel. *Wedding Dance.*

The dance continues.
Stops.

Song:
There was I,
Standing at the church, standing at the church,
Standing at the church.
There was I,
He'd left me in the lurch
My, how it did upset me.
Here's the note,
Here's the very note, here's the very note,
This is what he wrote.
Can't get away,
To marry you today,
My wife—won't let me!   *Music Hall Song*

Screen: Henri Cartier Bresson, photograph. *Sunday on the Banks of the Marne 1938.*
The group splits up into sections of three, four and five. Each group creates family activities—eating, walking, sitting together.

Screen: *Pictures of families.*

Voice: *Small boy*:
What did you do after dinner?
Voice *Self*:
The uncles sat in front of the fire, took off their collars, loosened all buttons, put their large moist hands over their watch-chains, groaned a little and slept. Mothers, aunts, and sisters scuttled to and fro, bearing tureens. The dog was sick. Auntie Beattie had to have three aspirins, but Auntie Hannah, who liked port, stood in the middle of the snow-bound back-yard, singing like a big-bosomed thrush. I would blow up balloons to see how big they would blow up to; and, when they burst, which they all did, the Uncles jumped and rumbled. In the rich and heavy afternoon, the uncles breathing like dolphins and the snow descending, I would sit in the front room, among festoons and Chinese lanterns, and nibble at dates, and try to make a model man-o'-war, following the Instructions for Little Engineers, and produce what might be mistaken for a sea-going tram. And then, at Christmas tea, the recovered uncles would be jolly over their mince-pies; and the great iced cake loomed in the centre of the table like a marble grave. Auntie Hannah laced her tea with rum, because it was only once a year. And in the

evening, there was Music. An uncle played the fiddle, a cousin sang 'Cherry Ripe', and another uncle sang 'Drake's Drum'. It was very warm in the little house. Auntie Hannah, who had got on to the parsnip wine, sang a song about Rejected Love, and Bleeding Hearts, and Death, and then another in which she said that her Heart was like a Bird's Nest; and then everybody laughed again, and then I went to bed.

Dylan Thomas. From Conversation about Christmas

Song:

O England was a free country
So free beyond a doubt
That if you had no food to eat
You were free to go without.

But if you want your freedom kept
You need to fight and strive
Or else they'll come and catch you, Jack,
And bind you up alive.

So rob their houses, tumble their girls,
Break their windows and all,
And scrawl your dirty words across
The whitewashed prison wall.

Voice *The Official*:
And up the stairs we're into the bedrooms. There's the two bedrooms, one big, one small; and there's your bathroom off the landing. You didn't have a bathroom down on the caravan site, did you? Mrs. Sawney! I say Mrs. Sawney; aren't you coming up to look at your bathroom? Oh come on missus, I haven't got all day. Blimey, you'd think I was showing you round a condemned cell or summat.

Voice *Rosie*:
Did you say it was a bathroom?

Voice *The official*:
God help us. Of course, love, I said it was a bathroom.

Voice *Sally*:
Bathroom? Is there water? Is there taps of water, mister?

Voice *Rachel*:
You shut your noise, Sally.

Voice *Rosie*:
Don't you go knocking her, she's not yourn, she's not yourn to go knocking her like that. *Sally howls.*
Shut your noise when you're told.

Voice *Official*:
Now look here, missus, do you want to see upstairs or don't you?

Voice *Rachel*:
Why? We've no choice, have we? You've put us to live here. Why can't we take our own bloody time looking at the place? So what if we *don't* like it. We've got no bloody choice.

Voice *Official*:
Eh God, I'm a reasonable man . . . *the baby cries.* But where did you get all this nonsense from, hey? 'No choice', 'put you to live here'—*who* put you to live here?

Voice *Rachel*:
You put us. Coppers put us—all the lot of narks.

Voice *Official*:
Now, wait, wait, I'm not the police, I mean look at me, Mrs. Sawney, did you ever see a policeman my shape of figure? All that's happened is: Your old place down by the caravans has had to be condemned, well, I mean: rightly—I mean a broken tramcar with no wheels nor windows, I wouldn't put pigs—all the rain coming in on you and all, why. . . .

Voice *Rachel*:
Our place, mister.

Voice *Official*:
But *this* is your place. *This* is your place.

John Arden. From Live Like Pigs

Voice:
My parents met at the Malvern Festival. Mum had gone over with friends, while father went to see the Shaw plays and the Barry Jackson productions, and he loved the theatre. They met and met again after Malvern and became engaged, and then both of them saved up until they could afford to get married. And then they were married, and Mum gave up teaching and moved into Northampton where they rented a house, still saving up enough to put down for a mortgage on a new house. They wanted a home more than anything else; a home fit to bring children into and give them every chance. They both made great sacrifices, and there was so much given up for the sake of the children that whenever I've gone off the conventional rails I have had terrible qualms, and had to argue it out with myself point by point whether I was doing the fair thing by them, what my reasons were.

Ray Gosling. From Sum Total

The group enter. They are wearing working clothes. They have tools and instruments. They proceed to show different kinds of work, with pick-axes, surgical instruments, typewriters, etc., etc.

Screen: *Succession of pictures of people working. Outdoor, indoor, in different parts of the world.*

Song:

When the farmer comes to town
With his wagon broken down,
Oh, the farmer is the man who feeds them all.
If you'll only look and see,
I think you will agree,
That the farmer is the man who feeds them all.

The farmer is the man
The farmer is the man
Lives on credit to the fall;
Then they take him by the hand,
And they lead him from the land,
And the middleman's the one who gets it all.

When the lawyer hangs around,
While the butcher cuts a pound,
Oh, the farmer is the man who feeds them all.
When the preacher and the cook
Go strolling by the brook
Oh, the farmer is the man who feeds them all.

The farmer is the man . . . (etc.).
When the banker says he's broke
And the merchant's up in smoke,
They forget that it's the farmer feeds them all.
It would put them to the test
If the farmer took a rest;
Then they'd know that it's the farmer feeds
them all.

The farmer is the man
The farmer is the man,
Lives on credit till the fall;
With the interest rate so high,
It's a wonder he don't die,
For the mortgage man's the one who gets it all.

American Song. 1890's

Voice:

If work isn't fun, don't do it.

Voice:

In a far-away northern country in the placid pastoral region,
Lives my farmer friend, the theme of my recitative, a famous tamer of oxen,
There they bring him the three-year-olds and the four-year-olds to break them,
He will take the wildest steer in the world and break him and tame him,
He will go fearless without any whip where the young bullock chafes up and down the yard,
The bullock's head tosses restless high in the air with raging eyes,
Yet see you! How soon his rage subsides—how soon this tamer tames him;
See you! on the farms hereabouts a hundred oxen young and old, and he is the man who has tamed them,
They all know him, all are affectionate to him;
See you! Some are such beautiful animals, so lofty looking;
Some are buff-colour'd, some mottled, one has a white line running along his back,
Some are brindled.
Some have wide flaring horns (a good sign)—see you! the bright hides,
See, the two with stars on their foreheads—see, the round bodies and broad backs,
How straight and square they stand on their legs—what fine sagacious eyes!
How they watch their tamer—they wish him near them—how they turn to look after him!
What yearning expression! how uneasy they are when he moves away from them;
Now I marvel what it can be he appears to them (books, politics, poems, depart—all else departs),
I confess I envy only his fascination—my silent illiterate friend,
Whom a hundred oxen love there in his life on farms,
In the northern country far, in the placid pastoral region.

Walt Whitman. *The Ox-Tamer*

Song:

Way, haul away,
We'll haul away together,
Way, haul away,
Haul away, Joe.
Way, Haul away,
We'll pull for better weather
Way, Haul away,
Haul away, Joe.

*As they sing, they are all hauling on an imaginary
rope. When they finish, they continue in silence. A
wind begins to rise. It gets louder, it gets bleaker.
A slow drum beat is heard. The drum beat gets
more ominous. They slowly stop working. It grows
dark. The wind and the drum continue. The
figures stop working. They sink to the ground.
Darkness. Wind. Drum.*
*Out of the darkness comes a sighing. A reed-piper
sounds. A few notes, and it dies. It is picked up
again. The drum matches it. Another instrument—
a saxaphone, or a clarinet. Quiet jazz fills the
darkness.*
*The light returns. People are moving to the music.
The jazz gets stronger. The group move together.*

Song:

It was one Sunday morning,
 Lawd, Lawd, Lawd!
The preacher went a-huntin'
 Lawd, Lawd, Lawd!
He carried 'long his shot gun.
 Lawd, Lawd, Lawd!
Well, 'long come a grey goose.
 Lawd, Lawd, Lawd!
The gun went off boo-boo
 Lawd, Lawd, Lawd!
And down come a grey goose.
 Lawd, Lawd, Lawd!

He was six weeks a-fallin'
 Lawd, Lawd, Lawd!
And my wife an' yo' wife
 Lawd, Lawd, Lawd!
They gave him a feather pickin'
 Lawd, Lawd, Lawd!
They was six weeks a-pickin'
 Lawd, Lawd, Lawd!
And they put him on to parboil.
 Lawd, Lawd, Lawd!

He was six weeks a-boilin'
 Lawd, Lawd, Lawd!
An' they put him on the table
 Lawd, Lawd, Lawd!
An' the knife wouldn't cut him
 Lawd, Lawd, Lawd!
And the fork wouldn't stick him
 Lawd, Lawd, Lawd!
And they throwed him in the hog-pen
 Lawd, Lawd, Lawd!
An' the hog couldn't eat him
 Lawd, Lawd, Lawd!
Aw—he broke the hog's teeth out.
 Lawd, Lawd, Lawd!

They taken him to the saw mill
 Lawd, Lawd, Lawd!
An' the saw wouldn't cut him
 Lawd, Lawd, Lawd!
Ah, he broke the saw's teeth out.
 Lawd, Lawd, Lawd!
An' the las' time I seed him
 Lawd, Lawd, Lawd!
He was flyin' across de ocean
 Lawd, Lawd, Lawd!
With a long string o' goslin's,
 Lawd, Lawd, Lawd!
An' they all goin' 'Quack, Quack'.
 Lawd, Lawd, Lawd!

American Slave-Work Song

*From this develops some improvised music with
strong jazz rhythms. These rhythms are taken up
by the group, who join in the improvisations. These
develop into stronger ('hotter') rhythms, until a
jumpy 'ragtime' music has taken over. The group
start to dance, with great zest, and turn the
movement into a carnival. Figures, streamers,
sounds, celebrations break out. The whole area is
alive with sound and colour. The whole scene is
alive with music, colour and movement. The music
develops into a fairground sound, and then into the
distorted noise that accompanies sea-side excur-
sions.*

Screen: *Pictures of people on holiday. At the
sea-side. Abroad. Smiling. Sun-tanned.
Watching cricket, football, boxing.
Dancing, drinking, listening to music.
Ballet, opera, plays.*

Before the Kick-Off.

The crowd put on long colourful scarves, hats, and have football rattles. The area is filled with the sound of rattles. They suddenly stop. The whole scene is still.

They chant: *A football chant.*

Voice:
What a Crowd,
Rattles buzzing like aggravated bees.
Policemen pulling kids out of the ground.
Flashes of light bursting out everywhere.
Children running onto the pitch for autographs.
The crowd swaying to and fro,
Like a piece of silk held in the wind.
The bright green pitch,
Clashing with the red and white of scarves and rosettes.
The men squabbling with each other about teams and players.
The Kop lets up a mighty roar,
Shouting the Liverpool chant,
As the teams come out.

Alan Jones. *Before the Kick-Off*

Voice *Herod*: Goodwill, great joy, peace upon earth—I do not believe they are altogether possible. But it is the business of good government to try to make them possible.

Herod the King. Herod the Great. Ruler of Judaea. To the west, the Roman Empire. To the east, the Persian Empire. In the middle, a small country in a very dangerous position. If I lean towards the east, I am afraid of invasion from Rome: if I lean towards Rome, then I shall be called upon to fight Persia. I would prefer to choose neither. But I had to choose Rome, because Rome rules Egypt, and it is from Egypt that we buy our corn. We are not self-supporting. *I* am not self-supporting. I have Roman officers in my army, Roman advisers in my palace, Roman spies in my department of state. . . .

The secretary rises from his seat and moves towards Herod. He notices this and immediately changes his tone to one of insincere political rhetoric.

The enormous friendship and generosity shown by the Roman people to the people of Judaea can only be repaid by continued loyalty and vigilance. The historic alliance between our two great nations must be for every citizen an eternal inspiration. Peace, prosperity, goodwill: one man carries them all on his back. If he falls down—

Voice *Angel—interrupting him in the tone of a palace official*: King Herod. There are three visitors to Jerusalem asking for an audience.

Voice *Herod—casually*: Where do they come from?

Voice *Angel*: Persia.

Voice *Herod—in alarm*: Eh? Where is my secretary?

Voice *Secretary*: Sir?

Voice *Herod*: What's this about Persia?

Voice *Secretary*: They are not an official delegation. They said they want a private audience. They would not state their business. One of them is African. Sir: I think we had better be careful. . . . Do you want to see them?

Voice *Herod*: Ah? Yes, I'll see them. But you stay in the corner and listen to what they say. You may have to send a report to Caesar to keep my name clear. Do you understand?

Voice *Secretary*: Yes. . . .

The Wise Men rise and the Secretary beckons them forward.

The king is waiting, gentlemen. Will you come this way?

They present themselves in front of Herod. The secretary steps back.

Voice *Herod*: Good morning.
Voices *Wise Men*: Your Majesty.

John Arden. From *The Business of Good Government*

The carnival develops. A Carnival King is carried in on a chair. The people cheer. They blow 'raspberries', throw streamers and confetti. There are trumpets and drums, dancing and jollity, coloured lights. People erect colourful soap boxes. They wear colourful rosettes. Others wearing rosettes listen to them.

Children march through the area chanting

Vote, vote, vote for So- and- so;
Punch old So-and-so in the eye;
When he comes to the door,
We will knock him on the floor,
And he won't come a-voting any more!

From *The Lore and Language of Schoolchildren* by I. and P. Opie

Sung to the tune of Tramp, Tramp, Tramp the boys are marching.

The whole Carnival, with 'King' and electioneers, freezes.

Voice:
I know no safe depository of the ultimate powers of society but the people themselves. . . .

Thomas Jefferson

Voice:
The history of all hitherto existing society is the history of class struggles.

Freeman and slave, patrician and plebeian, lord and serf, guildmaster and journeyman, in a word, oppressor and oppressed, stood in constant opposition to one another, carried on an uninterrupted fight that each time ended, either in a revolutionary re-constitution of society at large, or in common ruin of the contending classes.

Karl Marx and Friedrich Engels.
From *The Communist Manifesto, 1888*

Voice *Sarah*: All right! So I'm still a communist! Shoot me then! I'm a communist! I've always been one—since the time when all the world was communist. You know that? When you were a baby and there was unemployment and everybody was thinking so—all the world was a communist. But it's different now. Now the people have forgotten. I sometimes think they're not worth fighting for because they forget so easily. You give them a few shillings in the bank, and they can buy a television so that they think it's all over, there's nothing more to be got, they don't have to think any more! Is that what you want? A world where people don't think any more? Is that what you want me to be satisfied with—a television set?

Arnold Wesker. From *Chicken Soup with Barley*

Voice:

Socialism is an opinion as to how the income of the country should be distributed. . . . How much should you have and how much should your neighbours have? What is your answer. . . . The distribution of wealth is not a natural phenomenon. Clear your mind of the fancy with which we begin as children, that institutions under which we live, including our legal ways of distributing income and allowing people to own things, are natural, like the weather. They are not. Because they exist everywhere in our little world, we take it for granted that they have always existed and must always exist, and that they are self-acting. That is a dangerous mistake. They are in fact transient makeshifts; and many of them would not be obeyed, even by well-meaning people, if there were not a policeman within call and a prison within reach. They are being changed constantly by Parliament because we are never satisfied with them. Sometimes they are scrapped for new ones; sometimes they are altered sometimes they are simply done away with as nuisances. The new ones have to be stretched in the law courts to make them fit, or to prevent them from fitting too well if the judges happen to dislike them. There is no end to this scrapping and altering and innovating. New laws are made to compel people to do things they never dreamt of doing before. Old laws are repealed to allow people to do what they used to be punished for doing. Laws that are not repealed are amended and amended and amended like a child's knickers until there is hardly a shred of the first stuff left. At the elections some candidates get votes by promising to make new laws or to get rid of old ones, and others by promising to keep things just as they are. This is impossible. Things will not stay as they are.

Bernard Shaw. From *The Intelligent Woman's Guide to Socialism*

The Carnival scene breaks and the people sit in a circle

Voice:

'I ought to be chief,' said Jack with simple arrogance, 'because I'm chapter chorister and head boy. I can sing C sharp.'
Another buzz.
'Well then,' said Jack, 'I—'
He hesitated. The dark boy, Roger, stirred at last and spoke up.
'Let's have a vote.'
'Yes!'
'Vote for chief!'
'Let's vote—'
This toy of voting was almost as pleasing as the conch. Jack started to protest but the clamour changed from the general wish for a chief to an election by acclaim of Ralph himself. None of the boys could have found good reason for this; what intelligence had been shown was traceable to Piggy while the most obvious leader was Jack. But there was a stillness about Ralph as he sat that marked him out; there was his size, and attractive appearance; and most obscurely, yet most powerfully, there was the conch. The being that had blown that, had sat waiting for them on the platform with the delicate thing balanced on his knees, was set apart.
'Him with the shell.'
'Ralph! Ralph!'
'Let him be chief with the trumpet-thing.'
Ralph raised his hand for silence.
'All right. Who wants Jack for chief?'
With dreary obedience the choir raised their hands.
'Who wants me?'
Every hand outside the choir except Piggy's was raised immediately.
Then Piggy too raised his hand grudgingly into the air.
Ralph counted. 'I'm chief then.'

William Golding: from *Lord of the Flies*

Hogarth: The Election—Canvassing for Votes.

Voice:

Voting, as it is conducted in Britain, is looked upon as the climax of the democratic process. Because of its quasi-sacrosanct nature it merits rather more attention than it is sometimes given. The freedom of the voter to use his vote as he chooses, or not at all, is a feature of the system which can be taken for granted. Apart from this, the usual defence of the British method of voting is that it is simple, expedient, and, by and large, fair. The least controversial aspect of the system is its simplicity. All British subjects over the age of eighteen are allowed to vote, with certain self-evident exceptions such as peers, lunatics and various categories of law-breakers. On the appointed and well-publicised day the voter merely has to go to the polling-station and place a cross on the ballot-paper against the name of the candidate he favours. The choice will generally lie between two or three candidates; it would be unusual for there to be more than four candidates. The system needs little understanding, and the number of spoilt ballot papers is negligible. . . .

The real need is not for a change of voting system but for a realisation that three parties are one too many. As a means of choice between two parties the British system is excellent. It is simple; it does not require large multi-member constituences where contact between M.P.s and their constituents is likely to be lost; it is likely to produce a Government with a sound working majority. The ideal solution, therefore, would be the emergence of a single Radical party to oppose the Conservatives. The Conservatives represent one philosophy of government, the radicals in their different ways, another. But the latter can hardly do themselves justice while they are divided. . . .

> N. H. Brasher. From *Studies in British Government*

The people divide into two groups. They face each other. The King is pulled off his throne with a crash. Each group grabs hold of balloons and carnival festoons and look at each other menacingly. There is silence.
A light spills out over the area. The figures look up. They stagger, start to move slowly, jerkily. Balloons are burst, streamers fly up, sparks fly. Smoke fills the area. Figures leap. Sounds splutter. The carnival disintegrates in confusion and rebellion.

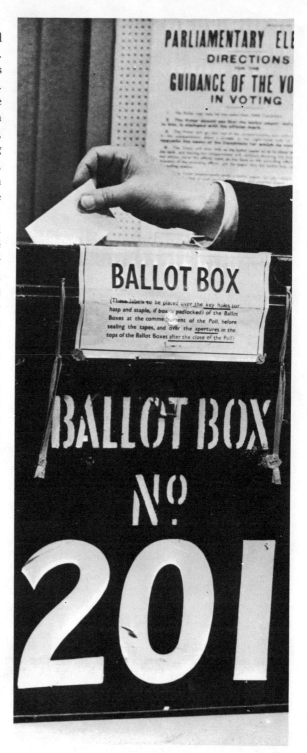

Voice:

And remember that thou wast a servant in the land of Egypt, and that the Lord thy God brought thee out thence through a mighty hand and by a stretched out arm: therefore the Lord thy God commanded thee to keep the sabbath day.

Honour thy father and thy mother, as the Lord thy God hath commanded thee; that thy days may be prolonged, and that it may go well with thee, in the land which the Lord thy God giveth thee.

Thou shalt not kill.

Voice:

Last night to the flicks. All war films. One very good one of a ship full of refugees being bombed somewhere in the Mediterranean. Audience much amused by shots of a huge fat man trying to swim away with a helicopter after him, first you saw him wallowing in the water like a porpoise, then you saw him through the helicopter's gun sights, then he was full of holes and the sea around him turned pink and he sank as suddenly as though the holes had let in water. Audience shouting with laughter as he sank.

George Orwell. From '1984'

There is an explosion. A roar of bullets. The battered carnival crowd stand alarmed. They look up. Clouds gather. The people scream. Bullets again. The people start to run. They herd together. They panic—pulling with them the carnival balloons and masks. The gunfire gets closer. They run away, clearing the carnival.

Screen: *War scenes. Wars in the middle ages. The first world war. Vietnam.*

Chorus:
　　Suppose that you have seen
The well-appointed king at Hampton pier
Embark his royalty; and his brave fleet
With silken streamers the young Phoebus fanning.
Play with your fancies; and in them behold
Upon the hempen tackle ship-boys climbing:
Hear the shrill whistle which doth order give
To sounds confus'd; behold the threaden sails,
Borne with th' invisible and creeping wind,
Draw the huge bottoms through the furrowed sea,
Breasting the lofty surge: O, do but think
You stand upon the rivage, and behold
A city on th'inconstant billows dancing;
For so appears this fleet majestical,
Holding due course for Harfleur. . . .
Work, work your thoughts, and therein see a siege;
Behold the ordnance on their carriages,
With fatal mouths gaping on girded Harfleur.
Suppose th' ambassador from the French comes
　　　　　　　　　　　　　　　　back;
Tells Harry that the king doth offer him
Katherine his daughter; and with her to dowry,
Some petty and unprofitable dukedoms.
The offer likes not; and the nimble gunner
With linstock now the devilish cannon touches. . . .
And down goes all before them.

From *Henry V*

There is another explosion

Song:

Up to your waist in water, up to your eyes in slush,
Using the kind of language, that makes the sergeant blush;
Who wouldn't join the army? that's what we all enquire,
Don't we pity the poor civilians sitting beside the fire.

Chorus:
Oh! Oh! Oh! It's a lovely war,
Who wouldn't be a soldier eh?
Oh! It's a shame to take the pay
As soon as reveille has gone
We just feel as heavy as lead,
But we never get up till the sergeant brings
Our breakfast up to bed.

Oh! Oh! Oh! It's a lovely war,
What do we want with eggs and ham
When we've got plum and apple jam?
Form fours! right turn!
How shall we spend the money we earn?
Oh! Oh! Oh! It's a lovely war.

J. P. Long and Maurice Scott. 1st World War Song

John Nash: Over the top.

Voice:
Helmet and rifle, pack and overcoat
Marched through a forest. Somewhere up ahead
Guns thudded. Like the circle of a throat
The night on every side was turning red.

They halted and they dug. They sank like moles
Into the clammy earth between the trees.
And soon the sentries, standing in their holes,
Felt the first snow. Their feet began to freeze.

At dawn the first shell landed with a crack.
Then shells and bullets swept the icy woods.
This lasted many days. The snow was black.
The corpses stiffened in their scarlet hoods.

Most clearly of that battle I remember
The tiredness in eyes, how hands looked thin
Around a cigarette, and the bright ember
Would pulse with all the life there was within.

Louis Simpson. *The Battle*

121

John Nash: Stand to before dawn.

122

The group are now dressed in sombre clothes. The gunfire dies. A bell tolls.
They stand.

Voice:
At five in the afternoon.
It was exactly five in the afternoon.
A boy brought the white sheet
at five in the afternoon.
A frail of lime made ready
at five in the afternoon.
The rest was death and death alone
at five in the afternoon.

The wind blew the cotton wool away
at five in the afternoon.
And the oxide scattered glass and nickel
at five in the afternoon.
Now the dove and the leopard fight
at five in the afternoon.
And a thigh with a desolate horn
at five in the afternoon.
Bourdon sounds struck up
at five in the afternoon.
Arsenic bells and smoke
at five in the afternoon.
At every corner hushed groups
at five in the afternoon.
And the bull alone exultant!
at five in the afternoon.
When the sweat of snow appeared
at five in the afternoon,
when the bullring was covered in iodine
at five in the afternoon, death laid eggs in the wound
at five in the afternoon.
At five in the afternoon.
At exactly five in the afternoon.

A coffin on wheels is his bed
at five in the afternoon.
Bones and flutes rung in his ears
at five in the afternoon.
Now the bull bellows on his forehead
at five in the afternoon.
The room became iridescent with agony
at five in the afternoon.
In the distance the gangrene now is coming
at five in the afternoon.
A lily-trumpet in his green groin
at five in the afternoon.

The wounds burned like suns
at five in the afternoon,
and the crowd was breaking windows
at five in the afternoon.
At five in the afternoon.
Ah, that dreadful five in the afternoon!
It was five by all the clocks!
It was the shadow of five in the afternoon!

Federico Garcia Lorca. From *Lament for Ignacio Sanchez Mejias* translated by J. L. Gili

The whole group sit in a circle. Cold light.

Voice:
Old woman, old woman, wilt thee gang a-shearin'?
Speak a little louder, I am very hard o' hearin'!
Old woman, old woman, wilt thee gang a-gleanin'?
Speak a little louder, or what's the use o' tawkin'?
Old woman, old woman, wilt thou let me kiss thee?
Yes, kind sir, and the Lord i' heav'n bless thee.

Traditional

Voice:
It is still quite light.
I have nothing to do but watch the days draw out,
Now that I sit in the house from October to June,
And the swallow comes too soon and the spring will be over
And the cuckoo will be gone before I am out again.
O sun, that was once so warm, O Light that was taken for granted
When I was young and strong, the sun and light unsought for
And the night unfeared and the day expected
And clocks could be trusted, tomorrow assured
And time would not stop in the dark!
Put on the lights. But leave the curtains undrawn.
Make up the fire. Will the spring never come? I am cold.

T. S. Eliot. From *The Family Reunion*

Voice:
The hump of a man bunching chrysanthemums
Or pinching-back asters, or planting azaleas,
Tramping and stamping dirt into pots—
How he could flick and pick
Rotten leaves or yellowy petals,
Or scoop out a weed close to flourishing roots,
Or make the dust buzz with a light spray,
Or drown a bug in one spit of tobacco juice,
Or fan life into wilted sweet-peas with his hat,
Or stand all night watering roses, his feet blue in rubber boots.

Theodore Roethke *Old Florist*

Voice:
Earth walks on Earth like glittering Gold;
Earth says to Earth, all's made of mould;
Earth builds on Earth, Castle and Towers,
Earth says to Earth, all shall be ours.

124

Voice:

A few light taps upon the pane made him turn to the window. It had begun to snow again. He watched sleepily the flakes, silver and dark, falling obliquely against the lamplight. The time had come for him to set out on his journey westward. Yes, the newspapers were right; snow was general all over Ireland. It was falling on every part of the dark central plain, on the treeless hills, falling soft upon the Bog of Allen and, farther westward, softly falling into the dark mutinous Shannon waves. It was falling, too, upon every part of the lonely churchyard on the hill where Michael Furey lay buried. It lay thickly drifted on the crooked crosses and head-stones, on the spears of the little gate, on the barren thorns. His soul swooned slowly as he heard the snow falling faintly through the universe and faintly falling, like the descent of their last end, upon all the living and the dead.

James Joyce. From *Dubliners*

Voice:

Sleep now,
Your blood moving in the quiet wind;
No longer afraid of rabbits
Hurrying through the tall grass
Or the faces laughing on the beach
And among the cold trees.

Sleep now,
Alone in the sleeves of grief,
Listening to clothes falling
And to your flesh touching God;
To the chatter and backslapping
Of Christ meeting heroes of war.

Sleep now,
Your words have passed
The lights shining from the East
And the sound of the flack
Raping graves and emptying seasons.

You do not hear the dry wind pray
Or the children play
A game called 'Soldiers' in the street.

Brian Patten, *Sleep Now*—in memory of Wilfred Owen

There is silence. The group slowly stand, put hands on each other's shoulders and turn.

Screen: *A graveyard.*

Silence. Still cold light.
The sound of a distant flute is heard, a lonely rising melody, growing louder.
The light grows brighter, warmer.

Voice:

'Rise up, my love, my fair one, and come away.
For lo, the winter is past, and the rain is over and gone;
The flowers appear on the earth; the time of the singing of birds is come, and the voice of the turtle is heard in our land;
The fig tree putteth forth her green figs, and the vines with the tender grapes give a good smell.
Arise my love, my fair one, and come away.'

From *The Song of Solomon*

The flute melody rises.
The people turn.

Screen: *A succession of pictures of children, young people.*

Children sing:

There was a man of double deed
Sowed his garden full of seed.
When the seed began to grow,
'Twas like a garden full of snow;
When the snow began to melt,
'Twas like a ship without a belt;
When the ship began to sail,
'Twas like a bird without a tail;
When the bird began to fly,
'Twas like an eagle in the sky;
When the sky began to roar,
'Twas like a lion at the door;
When the door began to crack,
'Twas like a stick across my back;
When my back began to smart,
'Twas like a penknife in my heart;
When my heart began to bleed,
'Twas death and death and death indeed.

From *The Oxford Book of Nursery Rhymes* compiled by I. and P. Opie

126

Children sing:
This is the key of the kingdom;
In that kingdom is a city,
In that city is a town,
In that town there is a street,
In that street there winds a lane,
In that lane there is a yard,
In that yard there is a house,
In that house there is a room,
In that room there is a bed,
On that bed there is a basket,
    A basket of flowers.

Flowers in the basket,
Basket on the bed,
Bed in the chamber,

Chamber in the house,
House in the weedy yard,
Yard in the winding lane,
Lane in the broad street,
Street in the high town,
Town in the city,
City in the kingdom:
    This is the key of the kingdom.
        From *The Oxford Book of Nursery Rhymes*
        compiled by I. and P. Opie

Screen: *Pictures of children walking and playing. Children from many lands. The group stand in complete silence. The light comes up to full. The screen holds a picture of a child.*

127

Acknowledgements

p. 8: Alan Vines, Report, London; p. 10: Camera Press; p. 14: Henry Grant; p. 19: Radio Times Hulton Picture Library; p. 21: Mary Evans Picture Library; p. 24: Radio Times Hulton Picture Library; p. 26: E. J. Fancy (Distributors); p. 28: Colin Blakely in the title role of the National Theatre production of Volpone by Ben Johnson; p. 31: Henry Grant; p. 32: Camera Press; p. 33: Barnaby's Picture Library; pp. 39, 41, 46, 48: Radio Times Hulton Picture Library; p. 51: The Hutchinson Publishing Group Ltd from The Railway Navvies by Terry Coleman; p. 55: J. Allan Cash; p. 61: Camera Press; p. 69: The Japanese Information Centre, London; p. 72: John John Spinner; p. 76: Titanus International; p. 79: John Spinner; pp. 83, 89: Dominic Photography; p. 95: Camera Press; p. 96: By courtesy of the Medici Society Ltd, London; p. 100: Fitzwilliam Museum; pp. 103, 104, 109, 111, 115: Camera Press; p. 118: The Trustees of Sir John Soane's Museum; p. 119: Camera Press; pp. 121, 122: The Imperial War Museum; p. 125: Camera Press; p. 127: Henry Grant.

The authors and publishers are indebted to Faber and Faber Ltd for extracts from 'Lord of the Flies' by William Golding, from 'The Family Reunion' by T. S. Eliot, and 'The Old Florist' from The Complete Poems of Theodore Roethke; J. M. Dent and Sons and the Trustees for the copyrights of the late Dylan Thomas for extracts from Letters to Vernon Watkins and 'Conversation about Christmas'; Laurence Pollinger Ltd, William Heinemann Ltd and the Estate of the late Frieda Lawrence for an extract from 'The Rainbow' by D. H. Lawrence; Macmillan, London and Basingstoke for an extract from 'Studies in British Government' by N. H. Brasher; John Murray Publishers Ltd for an extract from 'Indoor Games near Newbury' by John Betjeman; Methuen and Co. Ltd for an extract from 'The Business of Good Government' by John Arden; New Directions Publishing Corporation, New York for Lament for Ignacio Sanchez Mejias by Federico Garcia Lorca from Selected Poems, translated by J. L. Gili and Stephen Spender; Penguin Books Ltd for an extract from Live like Pigs by John Arden, © John Arden 1961; Charles Scribner's Sons, New York for Louis Simpson's 'The Battle' reprinted from Poets of Today II, Good News of Death and other poems, © Louis Simpson 1955; The Society of Authors and the Bernard Shaw Estate for an extract from The Intelligent Woman's Guide to Socialism; © IPC Magazines Limited 1970 for A Date to Remember reprinted from Valentine; George Allen and Unwin Ltd for 'Sleep Now' by Brian Patten, reprinted from 'Little Johnny's Confession'.

Every effort has been made to trace owners of copyright material, but in some cases this has not been possible. The publishers would be glad to hear from any further owners of material reproduced in this book.